BLOODY WELSH HISTORY

HISTORY

SWANSEA

GEOFF BROOKES

The
History
Press

To my children,
Laura, Catherine, Jennie and David.
The past is mine. The future is yours.

The History Press
The Mill, Brimscombe Port
Stroud, Gloucestershire, GL5 2QG
www.thehistorypress.co.uk

British Library Cataloguing in Publication Data.
A catalogue record for this book is available from the British Library.

ISBN 978 0 7524 8053 4

Typesetting and origination by The History Press
Printed in Great Britain

CONTENTS

ACKNOWLEDGEMENTS

I OWE A HUGE debt of gratitude to the unknown reporters of *The Cambrian*, Wales' first newspaper, who have provided me with enormous amounts of information – and entertainment. I have a lot of respect for the work they did and for their success in capturing the very essence of the times they lived in. Our understanding of the past would be so much poorer without them.

I must acknowledge the work of Ditta Szalkai, an amazingly talented artist from Hungary, who produced two excellent illustrations for me at very short notice. I am sure you will appreciate them as much as I do.

Of course there is also my nephew, Tom Sutton, who found the references I needed in the *Gesta Stephani*.

I am particularly indebted to the *South Wales Evening Post* for their permission to use *Memories of Swansea at War* (which allows the voice of real people who experienced those awful times to be heard), and for the reproductions of articles.

I must thank my friends at *Welsh Country Magazine* for permission to draw upon the article I wrote for them about the *Hecla*.

The staff at the Central Library in the Civic Centre in Swansea have been wonderfully patient with me, and the Swansea Archive Service are always helpful and accommodating in the face of my erratic and unstructured enquiries. I am very grateful for their permission to use the pictures which have made such a contribution to the book.

The Oxford University of Natural History has been very helpful; a model of generosity and scholarship.

I must also thank William Brookes, an itinerant chimney sweep, who was charged with stealing a quantity of herring in April 1834. It is good to know that I share a surname with someone who made an important contribution to the history of the town.

But most importantly I must acknowledge the greatest debt I owe and that is to my family, who have had to cope with someone who constantly drifts into the past at inopportune moments, avoiding all manner of jobs and responsibility. It is what I do best.

THE BULL MESMERISER   August 1850

———— ∞ ————

Mr Williams, the person who attempted to put a bull into a state of coma, has been obliged to have his leg amputated, in consequence of the injuries received.

———— ∞ ————

INTRODUCTION

I **AM NOT A** historian. Just a storyteller. My book tries to capture the story of the people who lived here before us, both for ourselves and for those who will follow us, from the very earliest times to 1947.

Today this is our city, our place. It is hard to think that what Dylan Thomas called our 'lovely ugly town' once belonged to others. They built it for us and we mustn't forget what they did. There are over a quarter of a million of us now, proud to live in the second city of Wales. It is not always a place that has lived in the full glare of history, but the curious group of people who have made Swansea their home over the centuries have made their own contribution to what the world is today. They have fought and argued, largely with each other, and in doing so have left such stories behind them. Stories of courage and desperation, unhappiness and achievement. These scenes from our history lie beneath our skin. This is what we are.

27,000 BC

THE RED LADY
OF PAVILAND

Gender Bender

IT IS APPROPRIATE, I think, that this skeleton history of Swansea should itself begin with a skeleton – and what a skeleton it is, the best-known prehistoric burial in Britain and the first human fossil ever found. But let's get one thing straight before we start. The Red Lady of Paviland was no lady. She was a man, and his discovery was initially littered with such misunderstandings.

Bones, believed to be those of elephants, had been found in Gower in December 1822. The discovery brought William Buckland, Professor of Geology at Oxford University, to the site at Goat's Hole in January 1823 and he unearthed the remains of an incomplete skeleton, stained red. It was bones from the right side of the body. The area around the body was also stained red, as were the items buried with the body – mammoth ivory bracelet fragments and perforated periwinkle shells. Small limestone blocks were uncovered, which might have been placed at the head and feet. The skull of a mammoth found nearby may also have been part of the burial ritual. Sadly, the skull has since been lost.

Strangely, Buckland chose to ignore all this evidence. His first assumption was that this was a customs officer murdered by smugglers – perhaps not that unreasonable, given the amount of smuggling that had taken place so recently. A decayed red jacket might explain the stains, too. His friend Lewis W. Dillwyn, later Lord Mayor of Swansea, moved the argument on when he wrote that 'these caves had once been places of concealment for a manufacturer of Celtic arrow heads and spears'.

When Buckland published his findings later in the year though, he had changed the story. Now he had decided that the ochre-stained skeleton was a 'painted lady', who entertained

The bones of the Red Lady of Paviland. (© Oxford University Museum of Natural History)

Goat's Hole is difficult and dangerous to reach. It is only really accessible at low tide and then only with extreme care. Formed by wave action, when the sea level was up to 8m higher than today, the cave entrance is pear-shaped. It leads on to a passage which extends for about 30m into the limestone cliff.

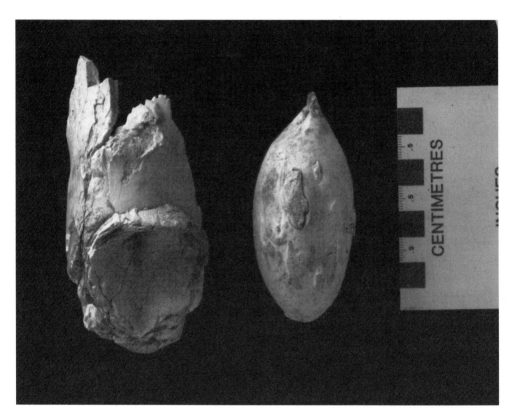

A pendant and tusk fragment found with the bones. (© Oxford University Museum of Natural History)

the Roman soldiers garrisoned in the camp on the hill above the cave. Alternatively, she could have been a witch.

The problem was that Buckland was entirely wrong. The burial was male, and the mammoth products were original and Palaeolithic and not manufactured at a later date as decorations. The camp was Iron Age, not Roman. Buckland's difficulty was that the historical record rather contradicted his own firmly held beliefs. He was a creationist and could not accommodate the idea that anything could pre-date the notional date of the Great Flood. Thus the body could not have been that old. It was on such a basis, neither scientific nor evidential, that he drew his conclusions. But the bits of bones that he found were very old indeed.

We now believe that the Red Lady was a ceremonial Palaeolithic burial dating from about 27,000 BC. Other examples have since been

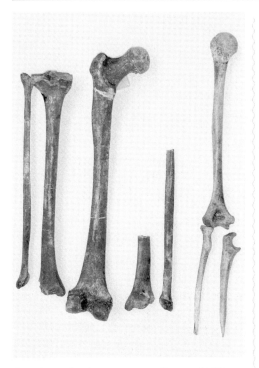

'Dem bones dem bones gonna walk around.' (© Oxford University Museum of Natural History)

found across Europe. The head of the Red Lady has never been found, though it was possibly removed as part of the burial. There are examples of this in similar graves from the period.

The Red Lady was a healthy young adult male, aged twenty-five to thirty, about 5ft 6in tall and weighing about 11 stone. The people he belonged to probably lived in a cold environment, appearing possibly like North American Indians or Inuit.

His world was different to ours. Gower was an impressive plateau, looking out over a vast plain of grassland which we now call the Bristol Channel. Herds of migrating animals would have followed age-old routes below the cliffs. So whilst the cave is now dangerously placed above the sea, at the time of the burial it would have been about 70 miles inland. Analysis indicates that the Red Lady lived on a diet that contained a significant proportion of fish, which, together with the distance from the sea, suggests that his people may have been semi-nomadic, or that the tribe had brought the body from the coast for burial in an important place. Naturally all this is complete guesswork. But it is a perfect example of the mysteries that lie beneath our feet, the residue from ancient alien times that is there if we look closely enough.

There have been earlier finds in the area. A stone axe, which may be 100,000 years old, was found at Rhossili. There are possibly more to be found. Gower has many caves which show evidence of our oldest ancestors. Indeed, the area has been constantly inhabited and you will find relics from every age: Stone Age, Iron Age, Bronze Age, Industrial Age. But nothing quite as important as the Red Lady has been found since.

And whilst she does go out on tour now and again and has been semi-permanently on display in the National Museum in Cardiff, her official home is in the University Museum in Oxford. You can see a replica of her in Swansea Museum but perhaps that is not quite enough. Perhaps she should come home. Druids want the remains returned to Swansea in order to 'balance the spiritual energies'. A good idea if you ask me.

Today you can paintball in Gower and cover yourself in red if you wish. The 'Red Lady' was a young adult male: an ideal paintballing client. Today he might pay to get covered in red paint, but never to such long-lasting effect as he did as the Red Lady of Paviland.

AD 43–74

DEATH ALONG THE BORDER!

Iron Age Battles and Roman Assaults

SWANSEA'S EARLY HISTORY was violent. Take nearby Hardings Down: a hump in the landscape at Llanmadoc, 500ft high, with prominent Iron Age earthworks. There are stories of a fierce battle there between local tribes, when Chief Tonkin was killed and the blood rose above the boots of the warriors. Mind you, the Welsh seem to have said that about every minor skirmish and battle, as we will see in another bloody encounter at Garngoch.

Iron Age Swansea was never a huge population. There were small tribes and families of nomads who came to Wales and left as the ice cap advanced. When it receded, farms and settlements were established during the Neolithic period. Their remnants are still there for us to see in Gower, in burial chambers like Parc le Breos.

The population increased with continental immigration in the Bronze Age (around 2000 BC). These ancestors spread more widely – there is evidence, for example, of a small settlement on Kilvey Hill. You can see slow progress towards greater sophistication in the Iron Age relics we have found. Easily accessible

The burial chamber at Parc le Breos, Gower. (Author's collection)

satellite images make the shadows they have left behind on the landscape available to us all. Look and you will see hill forts at Hardings Down or the Knave in Gower. As time went on, these small groups expanded and adopted greater social organisation and structure.

By the time the Romans came, the predominant tribe was a Celtic one called the Silures. The Romans described them as having a dark complexion and curly hair, and seemed to believe that they were recent immigrants from Spain. Wherever they came from, they certainly didn't like the Romans.

What did the Romans do for us? Well, not a great deal to be honest. They left a fine road running to Loughor and Carmarthen, a couple of small villas, and the occasional pile of coins here and there. But Swansea was never at the forefront of the Roman mind. They would march from Neath to Loughor and barely glance to the left as they did so. The estuary of the river Tawe had no importance at all. They were more interested in subduing a population.

When Emperor Claudius invaded Britain in AD 43, the tribes united under Togodumnus and his brother Caratacus, but they were quickly defeated by a highly experienced army. Caratacus fled to the west, where he found support from the tribes in Wales: the Ordovices and the Silures.

The Silures fought fairly constantly against the invaders. The Roman historian Tacitus described them as 'inferior in numbers but superior in cunning and knowledge of the country'. This knowledge was exploited by the tribe and was a constant irritant to the Romans. The Silures would pick off small groups, like cavalry detachments, without confronting the invaders in a pitched battle that they were always going to lose. Sensible tactics, but not ones the Romans appreciated. As far as they were concerned, they believed quite firmly that the Silures should be completely exterminated. Caratacus was eventually defeated at the Battle of Caer Caradoc on the Welsh border in AD 50, and his wife, daughter and brother were captured.

It was when Caratacus was banging on about cheese on toast that a senator looked at the piazza and had a really interesting idea.

Caratacus fled again but Cartimandua, the Queen of the Brigantes, betrayed him and he was taken to Rome for celebratory execution. However, he gave a speech which persuaded the Emperor to spare him and his family, in which he is said to have remarked, 'Why do you, with all these grand possessions, still covet our poor huts?' An opinion which summarised a world view that has been a constant theme throughout history.

By AD 74 the Silures were finally subdued by the governor Julius Frontinus. Whether they had been defeated in battle or reached a peaceful compromise isn't known, but the south of Wales settled down to a period of peace.

As they did everywhere, the Romans imposed themselves on the landscape. They built roads and forts across the region from their base in Caerleon. The remains of military structures have been found in Neath and Loughor, along the road that ran to Moridunum (Carmarthen). Forts were mostly found at regular intervals, separated by a day's march, so it is unlikely that there was anything of great significance in the Swansea area, although there may have been a Roman camp on Garngoch Common.

So many kebabs, so little time. (By kind permission of the Thomas Fisher Rare Book Library, University of Toronto)

The fact that the Roman legacy in Wales does not go much further than roads and fortifications indicates that Wales was a country under military occupation. Furthermore, there are few examples of Latin words being absorbed into Welsh. The Latin for *window* is *fenestra*, which relates obviously to the Welsh word *ffenestr*, but it is as if the two cultures lived separate lives: one on the road and the other off it.

The Via Julia Maritima was a coastal road which passed through parts of Swansea. You can still see its outline if you stand on Middle Road in Fforestfach and look down the hill along the A4070 to Gorseinon. The road crossed the river Tawe. When a lock was built on the Tawe to serve the pottery works down where Sainsbury's is now, a paved crossing was found several feet below the existing riverbed.

There is some evidence of Roman farmsteads in Gower and it appears that Mumbles may have been famous for its oysters. There is another, more prosaic, explanation that the name

Oystermouth is the nearest an English tongue could get to the Welsh name Ystumllwynarth. But it is important to preserve a sense of romance and certainly Roman artefacts have been found there. For example, bits of a mosaic were found in All Saints' churchyard; these are collectively known as the Saints' Pavement. A seventeenth-century historian, Isaac Hamon, believed that a group of men had lived in a cave and spent their time making small bricks of 'divers colours' in order to pave the churchyard. A harmless, if odd, hobby, though as a theory it is entirely wrong; however, in principle men could have lived in a cave making bricks all day long, since Swansea was largely a peaceful place in those days – apart from occasional raiders, usually from Ireland.

Buried coins have also been unearthed. There have been discoveries at Llandarcy, on the beach at Port Tennant, and in the Uplands. The Pennard hoard of over 2,000 coins was found in 1966 when a septic tank was being dug. The Gwindy hoard was found below Pentrechwyth near Morfa in 1835. A local girl discovered the treasure by a stream when the coins were exposed following a thunderstorm. The news was 'noised abroad' and 'a number of persons' descended upon it, pulling out the coins. They dated from the third century AD. It is reported that there were bones too. It is likely that it was a grave but, in their haste to get at the gold, the locals threw all the bones away and smashed the pottery container that held many of the coins. Forensic archaeology has never had much of a following in Pentrechwyth.

Broken pottery and abandoned coins have been unearthed on Wind Street too. Nothing new there, though. It merely goes to show that history is always keen to repeat itself.

AD 500s

ST CENYDD

A Boy and his Birds

THE CHURCH IN Llangennith in Gower is dedicated to our very own saint – St Cenydd. What we can see today is built on the site of a sixth-century priory founded by the saint himself, which was destroyed by Vikings in 986 – a bit unnecessary, considering everything that St Cenydd had done. His was quite a journey. Cenydd was fed by seagulls, brought up by angels and had a shocking limp, but then the boy did come from a particularly dysfunctional family.

He was born in unfortunate circumstances. His father was Dihoc, a prince of Brittany, and his mother was his sister, if you see what I mean. Yes, I am afraid to say that Dihoc seduced his own daughter. Now, King Arthur's Christmas party that year was in Gower, and Dihoc and his daughter were invited. But she proceeded to give birth to a son and his unnatural conception was displayed for all to see in his crippled leg. In order to hide this guilty secret, the baby was placed in a wicker cradle (rather like Moses, you might think) and cast adrift on the river Lliw.

The poor child drifted out into the estuary but was saved from disaster by the seagulls who rescued him and carried him away to Worm's Head. They stood around him in great flocks, with their wings outspread to protect him from the weather. An angel then turned up with a breast-shaped bell through which he was fed. This was called the Titty Bell. Honestly.

When a farmer found the baby and took him home, the gulls ripped the thatch from the roof (with the same sort of enthusiasm with which they attack our bin bags) and took him back to the nest. There, a doe kept the Titty Bell replenished. Cenydd's clothes grew along with him. If you could manage that with school uniform, you'd make a fortune. The angel kept popping back now and then to complete Cenydd's education, like some sort of divine home tutor.

When he was eighteen he went to Llangennith, where a spring emerged instantly; it was there that he built his retreat, where he had frequent meetings with the angels. Just a normal eighteen year old, I suppose. The Titty Bell was particularly useful, since it gave him the power to restore stolen property to the original owner and to convert thieves. It is such a shame that it has subsequently been misplaced.

St Cenydd's Church in Llangennith.
(Author's collection)

13

After its destruction by the Vikings, the priory in Llangennith was re-established when the Normans took possession of Gower. The income from the priory was used by Henry V to provide a pension to a loyal knight called Sir Hortonk van Klux and, with a name like that, it was the least he deserved. But he was honoured in another way too. It seems to me that St Cenydd's seagulls honour Sir Hortonk van Klux by calling out his name along the sea front all day long.

He became a friend of St David, who cured Cenydd of his disability so that he could attend a religious conference, the Synod of Brefi, in 545. However, Cenydd preferred to remain as he was born and prayed for a restoration of his condition. Clearly he didn't want to be accused of benefit fraud.

Every year, on 5 July, Llangennith held a celebration in his memory. The Mapsant, as it was known, was a festival of prize fights, cock fighting and dances. A particular delicacy was 'whitepot' – flour, milk and meat boiled together. Personally I think the recipe needs a bit more work but apparently it was to show respect for the Titty Bell. The party went on for three days and a wooden cock dressed in ribbons was hoisted to the top of the church tower to honour the birds that fed him.

The tomb of St Cenydd. (Author's collection)

AD 850

THE VIKINGS

A Rose by Any Other Name

THEY CAME TO call, of course they did. Swansea Bay was always a wide and attractive inlet. Despite this, there was never a major Viking settlement here, perhaps never anything more than a trading post. Their attentions were evidently drawn elsewhere – but it is hard to know where, since their interests didn't always extend as far as writing things down. They sought out more physical pleasures, generally.

Vikings normally came from the east, but, as they were repelled by Alfred the Great and then King Brian Boru in Ireland, they eventually turned their attentions to North Wales and to the north side of the Bristol Channel. But the pickings were much poorer and the sea more unpredictable. Meetings between the Welsh and the Vikings were often violent. Surviving fragments

He understood that it was his duty to resist Viking aggression but he still missed his life as a waiter. (www.fromoldbooks.org)

It was being captured in your pyjamas that was the most humiliating thing. (www.fromoldbooks.org)

of poetry proclaim that 'there will be heads split open without brains', a tradition much revived today in Swansea on a Friday night.

The first recorded attack was in 850 in the north, when a man called Cyngen was strangled. However, Viking activity was sporadic, with generally low-level confrontations – though not so low level if you were involved yourself. Often, as a contemporary chronicler put it, 'they returned laden to the ships, more heavily weighed down by their crimes than loaded with burdens'.

The British certainly regarded them as brutal and bloodthirsty, which has helped to seal their reputation in history. But on the whole they seem to have known little about Wales –

15

or Bretland, as they called it – and made little impact. They left little behind them, apart from a small hoard of coins found in Penrice and, perhaps most important of all, the name of our town – Swansea.

The town has had many different names over the centuries, including Sweynesse, Swaynsey, Swinesey and Svenesya, and there is no agreement about where the name came from. There is little doubt that the first part of the name – Sveinn – is Norse. What the second part means is the subject of some debate, in certain circles. Is it derived from the word *ey*, meaning island? After all, the river Tawe did split in two

'You worry about the spelling, I'll do the pillaging.' (Author's collection)

Our Viking heritage is remembered and honoured by the prows of the boats that emerge from the tower of the Guildhall. (Author's collection)

as it reached the sea. As to the first part, perhaps there was a trading post on this island run by a man called Sveinn. And who was he? Was he the brother of Harold, who was killed at the Battle of Hastings? Or is it in fact a reference to King Swanus, who had a fleet of ships that were lost in a storm at 'Swannawick' or 'Swansesey'? Or is it a reference to Sweyn Forkbeard? Or Swein, son of Aslief, from Orkney, who besieged Lundy for reasons best known to himself? We don't know. All we can say is that the survival of such a Norse name implies that the place wasn't a Welsh settlement originally, and nor did it become one for quite a while. But the name Swansea is the only surviving legacy of the Viking years.

AD 500–1100

THE DARK AGES

A Cow Economy

THE CONTROL AND order that the Romans had exerted quickly disappeared. The society they had created became fragmented and the area was controlled by chiefs and warlords. There were frequent and significant incursions by Irish raiders and settlers, and the family trees for the princes of Wales start to include Irish names at this time. The old certainties of Roman rule were replaced by poverty and confusion, and the economy based upon Roman consumer goods had largely disappeared.

Generally, it was not a happy time to be alive. In 535, a volcanic eruption in the Far East spewed so much ash into the air that a nuclear winter followed. The temperature dropped. There was little sunshine, crops failed and there was famine. And then seven years later bubonic plague arrived. The number of dead bodies that resulted from that led to outbreaks of cholera.

During this period, slavery was quite normal. Many were slaves by birth, though some may have been captives. There is a record of a Saxon woman being given in part payment for land. It might have been a bargain, but who can say? Generally, the going rate was fixed at one slave to four cows and eventually, though much later,

the value of a cow was fixed at 5s. As you might guess, Roman coins had long since gone. The economy operated through barter.

In fact, in the seventh century the cow was the measure of all things. The life of a householder was valued at between 126 and 252 cows. It was a very tribal society and it was really important to know who you belonged to.

A bull market is always an exciting time for investors. (By kind permission of the Thomas Fisher Rare Book Library, University of Toronto)

The main road to Swansea appears to have changed during this period. The Roman road was replaced by a route which went through Llansamlet, crossed the river at Morriston, and went to Llangyfelach, where there was a monastery which had a guesthouse.

In the *Mabinogion*, a collection of folk tales compiled in medieval times, there is a story, 'The Dream of Rhonabwy', which is set at about the time of the Norman Conquest. In it there is a description of a homestead. Is this perhaps how our ancestors lived? Or is it just a medieval view of how they thought they lived?

They saw an old hall, very black and having an upright gable, whence issued a great smoke; and on entering, they found the floor full of puddles and mounds; and it was difficult to stand thereon, so slippery was it with the mire of cattle. And where the puddles were, a man might go up to his ankles in water and dirt. And there were boughs of holly spread over the floor whereof the cattle had browsed the sprigs. When they came to the hall of the house, they beheld cells full of dust and very gloomy and on one side an old hag making a fire. And whenever she felt cold she cast a lapful of chaff upon the fire and raised such a smoke that it was scarcely to be borne, as it rose up the nostrils.

To be honest, it sounds a bit like where those relatives of yours live. You know, the ones you don't like visiting at Christmas.

In that sense it isn't much different in Swansea today. The responsibility for crimes like murder fell upon the extended family. Everyone had to contribute to the compensation to avoid a feud. Likewise, a family would share in any recompense received.

But in spite of such arrangements to minimise conflict, the different kingdoms of Wales were often at war. Swansea was on the frontier between two kingdoms, Deheubarth and Morgannwg, which is always a dangerous place to be. In the chronicle of Caradoc of Llancarfan, it is said that Einon, Prince of Deheubarth, 'pillaged the land of Gwyr and spoiled and devastated it so cruelly that a famine ensued'.

There was a particularly vicious battle in 970 when Einon fought near Cadle. We know few details of the encounter but it must have been significant because that is where Cadle gets its name from – it means 'place of battle'. In fact, other places have a connection with this momentous and largely forgotten battle – Penllergaer (the head of the camp) and Killay (the place of retreat). Einon was defeated and fled, being unhorsed and killed in a bog near Penllergaer. The truth, though, is very hard to determine. Another story suggests that in the battle at Cadle the leader of the western tribes, Llyn Cadwgan, was killed whilst drinking at a well close to the Roman road at Llewitha Bridge, Fforestfach. The well was Ffynnon Circonan or Colcona and is still visible today. I have been very fortunate to have had the opportunity to see it, deep within the brambles on private land, as cold and clear as ever. And the name of the place on the map? Llyn Cadwgan.

Cadwgan's men fled in confusion to cross the Loughor and were defeated for a second time on Garngoch Common (meaning 'red stones or hooves'). As we will see, it was not the only battle to be fought in those fields. But as the Welsh continued to fight each other, the Normans moved into Gower and Swansea.

Ffynnon Circonan. (Author's collection)

AD 1066–1116

WHEN THE NORMANS CAME

THERE ARE THREE turning points in the history of Swansea and this is the first of them – the arrival of the Normans following the Battle of Hastings in 1066 and the defeat of Saxon England.

The Normans appear to have arrived in the area from the sea, across the Bristol Channel. This explains two things about Gower. Firstly, it accounts for the number of castles along the south side, which is where they made their landings; secondly, it explains why that side has always been the English side. Look at the names and compare them to those in the north of Gower: Horton, Parkmill, Oxwich and then Penclawdd, Llangennith and Llanrhidian.

The Normans did not march through Wales and so they were perhaps insulated from the reality of the nation they had invaded. The Welsh found themselves conquered and colonised by a foreign military aristocracy who seized the best land. They therefore retreated

Penrice Castle. (By kind permission of the West Glamorgan Archive Service)

to the less comfortable uplands of the north. The two communities were separated by the common land that ran across the peninsula, though there was a Norman presence in the north too.

But it wasn't all bad. The Welsh, who for many centuries had had to make do with fighting each other, now had the chance to fight the Normans. They could at last unite in the face of a common enemy. It was not an opportunity to be wasted. These unpopular invaders and oppressors created a fairly constant state of war. It is noticeable, for example, that the oldest churches in the area generally date from the late twelfth and thirteenth centuries, probably because the Welsh destroyed all the earlier ones.

The Abbot of Gloucester wrote to a prior in Wales offering advice about the natives: 'Strengthen the locks on your doors and surround your house with a wall lest the people who gaze at you with shaggy brows and fierce eyes break in.'

Weobley Castle, Gower. (Author's collection)

This suggests that he had a somewhat jaundiced view of those to whom he should have offered spiritual guidance. There is also a sense of exclusion in these words – the idea that this new society could find no place for those who had always lived there. Early landowners had names such as Godafridus and Ricardus filius Segeri. One of the first toll collectors was Adam Croyland. These are not Welsh names.

The Welsh lived almost entirely away from the town which had developed outside the walls of the castle, obviously to cater for the garrison. Initially there were bakers, brewers and butchers; other merchants soon followed. But always trade and business were in the hands of the Normans and the English. The Welsh were not part of the new social order.

The first recorded lord was Henry de Beaumont, Earl of Warwick, and the symbol of his authority was the castle built above the Tawe. Originally it was turf and timber, which made it quick to erect. However, it remained rather vulnerable and neither permanent nor imposing, particularly when the locals were so keen on burning it down. It was certainly in a good position though. It was constructed on a small rise on what is now the city centre, overlooking the river below. It was a little further up the hill than the remains of the more recent castle, and probably stood where Worcester Place is today.

You can see the slope as you approach through Castle Square or up from the Strand, which, as you can tell from the name, is where

Death arrives for the Abbot of Gloucester, who advised that all Englishmen 'strengthen the locks on your doors!' (By kind permission of the Thomas Fisher Rare Book Library, University of Toronto)

the river originally ran until it was redirected. Strip the buildings away in your mind and you will get a sense of the underlying landscape.

The town was essentially a Norman place and the Welsh attacked it regularly. After all, the castle was a symbol of a foreign military power, subjecting a people who were not too happy about it. Gruffydd ap Rhys attacked it first in 1116, and probably Oystermouth Castle too. According to Giraldus Cambrensis, he 'burnt it outright and slew many within it'. The Welsh quickly adapted their military tactics, developing their longbows to penetrate Norman armour. They probably used fire arrows to set alight the wooden walls and buildings of the castle.

The town of Swansea was burnt on many occasions. In fact, the garrison once burnt the town themselves to deny the Welsh any cover as they approached the castle. In the end, it wasn't a surprise that the next lords of Swansea, the de Breos family, built a new castle, this time of stone. Nothing else in these times of trouble would do. And the castle is important, because it is with the building of the castle that our story starts to centre more completely upon the current city boundaries.

William the Conqueror, whose forces attacked South Wales in this era.

AD 1136

THE BATTLE OF LLWCHWR

WHAT DO YOU want to call it? The Battle of Llwchwr? The Battle of Penllergaer? The Battle of Garngoch? It has been called all these things, but really it doesn't matter what you call it. The reality is that it was a monumental battle in Welsh history and yet little is known about it. It shaped Wales for the next 150 years and it happened here, in Swansea.

Swansea in the twelfth century was a place under enemy occupation. The Welsh were strangers in their own land. Invaders had turned their world into deer parks like Parc le Breos and Clyne. The Beaumonts had controlled the area for about eighty years. Henry Beaumont was succeeded by Roger, who was 'more addicted to pleasure than gifted with courage' and was a 'handsome waster of his possessions', according to *The Red Book of Hergest*. He actually mortgaged the whole of Gower, which meant that it eventually became Crown property. This was not a well-respected family noted for its philanthropy, and Welsh princes were hardly going to accept the supremacy of such hollow and unimpressive rulers.

The first incursion by the Welsh into Gower happened in 1116. They could not at this stage face the Normans in open battle or take and hold a castle. But they could conduct guerrilla warfare – and they were very good at it. However, their opportunity for something more organised came on 1 January 1136, when the fight for independence suddenly had a focus.

The death of Henry I in Normandy, on 2 December 1135, has gone down in legend.

He died of food poisoning, allegedly from eating a surfeit of lampreys. How many of the creatures made up a 'surfeit' isn't clear but not only was it an unusual way to go, it also had significant consequences. With no clear successor, the country entered what was called 'The Anarchy' and the Welsh took advantage of the power vacuum. They gathered together under Hywel ap Maredudd, the Lord of Brycheiniog (Brecon), and advanced towards Gower, where apparently 'everything is delightful, fertile and luxuriant'. Not for long. They were joined by the Welsh from north Gower, who maintained a simmering grievance.

The stone marking the site of the battle on Garngoch Common. (Author's collection)

HENRY I

Coin of Henry I.

As far as the Norman chroniclers were concerned (and you can see this if you read Chapter Eight of the *Gesta Stephani*, their history of the period), the Normans were mightily offended by this sort of attitude. They saw it as a betrayal, after all they had done for the Welsh. They had introduced civilisation once 'they had vigorously subdued its inhabitants' and encouraged peace by 'imposing law and statutes'. How ungrateful could they be?

The Normans came out to meet the Welsh, expecting to confront a disorganised rabble whom they could quickly prevent from forming small raiding parties that would 'clear the villages by plunder, fire and sword', burning houses and slaughtering men. However, this was a significant force, as they found out when they met at Garngoch Common on New Year's Day 1136. The Normans, suddenly surrounded, formed themselves into a wedge but could not force their way through the Welsh. The battle was brutal and unforgiving. The Normans were bogged down in the mud and unable to move or to deploy. They were 'laid low with the edge of the sword'. It is said that 516 Normans were killed and their corpses eaten by wolves and birds.

Such a victory unleashed all the fury of a suppressed people. Gruffydd ap Rhys, Prince of Deheubarth (now west Wales), joined in and it became a full-scale revolt.

Rejoicing greatly at this first success in their insurrection they streamed boldly over every quarter of Wales; addicted to every crime, ready for anything unlawful, they spared no age, showed no respect for any order, were not restrained from wickedness either by time or place. (*Gesta Stephani*)

It gives you a warm glow of pride, doesn't it, to realise that the traditions of a rugby team on tour have such distinguished origins.

This victory gave the Welsh the belief that they could defeat the Normans, and fuelled rebellion for at least the next 150 years. Land changed hands regularly and Swansea was repeatedly attacked and destroyed. But they never succeeded in driving out the Normans. They might have defeated them here and there, but they never expelled them.

This encounter in 1136, however, has seeped into the landscape, in a triangle just beyond Tesco in Fforestfach. There is a stand of trees, for example, on Bryn Dafydd Farm. Tradition says that within the mound was a burial chamber and it was here that the Welsh set up their command post to direct the battle.

A memorial has been erected just along Hospital Road, off the old Roman road that we now call the B4620, to mark this moment in history. Parking isn't easy but there is a sign pointing to a rough track you can follow through the grass, still muddy, still boggy. At the far end of the field is a wonderful standing stone bearing the date 1136. It is still a bleak place, untouched by the modern world which surrounds Garngoch. And almost 1,000 years ago it was a cold place to die on New Year's Day.

SWANSEA, THE TOWN OF OPPORTUNITY

BEAUMONT OPERATED LARGELY as a king, able to try people for offences which in England could only be dealt with by the Crown. In fact, due to a possible shortage of coins, he minted his own. The Normans were an occupying force with no affinity for the place where they lived. They were merely there to exploit the resources which were often transferred overseas. So the tithes (or taxes) from some churches were transferred to Evreux in Normandy, and those from Llanrhidian and Landimore were used to treat sick pilgrims in the Holy Land.

As invaders, they established a defensive position on a rise above the river, and the geography that originally appealed to them hasn't gone. But there had to be convincing and sustainable economic reasons for choosing to settle in such a volatile place. There had to be incentives.

The original course of the river ran close to the Strand, curving from below High Street station down to where Sainsbury's is now, and flowed out into Fabian's Bay. Merchants could unload their cargoes close to the castle, trade for the hides and wool that came in from the surrounding area, and pretend to feel secure whilst doing so. They were encouraged to become burgesses of the town, with the offer of a plot of land for an annual rent of 12*d*. They also had rights to more land 'beyond the woods' which surrounded the town, where they could keep pigs and cattle, near Pentregethin Road in Port Mead. They could take oak for fences, ships and for fire. They had fishing rights too.

As far as shipwrecks were concerned, anything in the bay would be split between the Earl and the burgesses, but any that hit the shore were his alone. All very appealing incentives, I am sure, and perhaps you would be rushing

'I don't mind paying the fine. He wouldn't behave so I slapped him.' (By kind permission of the Thomas Fisher Rare Book Library, University of Toronto)

> The earliest form of the modern name of the town is recorded in 1160, when it is called Sweynesse. After a while it became Sweyse but, to the envy of inattentive schoolboys across the city, spelling was no way near as standardised as it is today. To be frank, you could get away with anything that looked vaguely close.
>
> But nothing could alter the fact that the town was slap-bang in the middle of a hostile environment. Sweyse (and its castle) was the administrative headquarters of a new order and it looked out across the river to Cilfai (Kilvey), where the people were entirely Welsh-speaking. They could see it pointing to a future that they did not like much.

to join them yourself – though let us remember that any sturgeon or porpoise belonged to the Earl. And also don't forget that the natives were particularly unfriendly, probably because they were told that none of the land was their own any longer.

As part of the deal, as a burgess you were expected to fight for the Earl – at your own expense if you could get home at the end of the day. But don't worry, it was at the Earl's expense if he led you further away. So basically, you could get out there into the Badlands, slap a few Welsh heads and then get home for a fish supper and a good night out.

It is interesting to see in the records that behaviour in the town was no better than it is now. 'Whoever shall shed blood from noon on Saturday to Monday morning shall be fined 40 shillings. And from Monday to Saturday 12 pence.' Of course, the Welsh themselves didn't generally live in towns and so they could not be blamed for such loutishness. They were tribal, protecting first and foremost the extended family with whom they lived. A residue of this is still seen in Welsh attitudes today. The first question of a stranger is always, 'Who do you belong to?'

The Normans, however, were not here for such family connections. They saw the potential for redevelopment and commercial exploitation. And so, whilst the Welsh tribes were arguing with each other, the Normans turned their attentions to the plentiful wood, water, deer, boar, salmon, porpoise and sturgeon. If you could avoid arguing with your neighbour's cousin, this was good, productive land.

IN TIMES OF TROUBLE

WILLIAM DE BREOS was vicious and uncompromising. One of the lasting impressions he left on the town was the rebuilding of the castle out of stone, where we can see the ruins today. It still overlooked the slope down to the quayside on the river. It had towers and castle walls which ran down to Caer Street, across Castle Gardens and up College Street.

Other destroyed castles were never rebuilt, like the one at Bishopston. But others were, such as Oystermouth and Pennard. Churches at Llanrhidian and Cheriton were developed into defensive positions, where people could shelter from Welsh attacks. It was still a settlement under threat and the defences of the town were improved too.

On the east side was a slope that ran down to the river. A wall on the top added to the sense of security. On the south side there was a stream called The Pill, along which a wall was built (down towards the bottom of Wind Street). On the west side there was another stream, called Town Ditch, which ran just beyond St Mary's Church, where the Quadrant is today. They dug a ditch along the north side. Wooden palisades were erected, to be replaced by stone walls. Their

Swansea Castle. (Author's collection)

Oystermouth Castle. (Author's collection)

Edward I on his way to Oystermouth Castle.
(www.fromoldbooks.org)

construction was paid for by a toll ('murage') on goods coming into the town. The main thoroughfare was Wind Street and High Street, with a gate at either end. The market place was at the top of Wind Street, at the junction with St Mary's Street.

The construction of such a defensive position indicates the constant sense of revolt and war. The Welsh were increasingly successful, especially when they united under Llewelyn, Prince of Wales. These were difficult times. However, by the end of 1283 Edward I had established English dominance across Wales. The death of Llewelyn, at Cilmery near Builth in 1282, left a vacuum which could not be filled. So in 1284 Edward made a royal tour of Wales as a symbol of his dominance, and in December he stayed at Oystermouth Castle as a guest of William de Breos.

AD 1289

JUST HANGING AROUND IN SWANSEA

BUT THE WELSH hadn't finished. On 27 June 1287, Oystermouth was taken and burnt in the rebellion of Rhys ap Maredudd, the Lord of Ystrad Tywi, who had once been an ally of Edward but now felt rather overlooked. As a contemporary chronicler would have it: 'Certain men who were captured Rhys caused to be strangled before his eyes, others he led away captive. He violated the church for the sake of loot and slew the wives and children of the men indifferently.'

He burnt Swansea to the ground and 'took away much spoil' – but it didn't do him any good because, when his uprising failed, he was captured and taken to Edward in York in 1292, where he was hanged and drawn as a traitor. But our local interest focuses on another individual involved in the uprising who, in 1289, was captured, imprisoned and executed – but managed to survive. This is the remarkable story of William ap Rhys, known to his friends as 'Crach', which translates as William the Scabby. Don't you just love it?

To be honest, he wasn't as popular as his name might suggest. He was described as a thief, an arsonist and a murderer. Crach was not very happy either. He was carrying a bit of baggage, you might say, since he had had his land in Llanrhidian confiscated by de Breos. He was about forty-five and was Welsh-speaking which, when combined with his other qualities, didn't really help his relationship with de Breos. Crach was accused of being a leader of the rebels who had destroyed Oystermouth Castle. He was apprehended in Gower and imprisoned in Swansea Castle for fifteen days, accused of killing thirteen men. His protestations of innocence were rejected and he was sentenced to death by hanging.

Oystermouth Castle never really recovered. The castle as it is today. (Author's collection)

On 11 November 1289, he was taken from prison to the gallows sited on what we call North Hill, between Seaview School and Dyfatty Street. He was not alone, for he was to be executed along with Trahaearn ap Hywel from Llangyfelach, who was regarded as a brigand and a murderer. An offer of 100 cows had been made by an unknown supporter to buy a reprieve for them both, but this was rejected. Lady Mary de Breos begged for leniency, but her husband rejected her pleas and so instead she asked for possession of William's body once he was dead.

The condemned were marched up to the gallows under close escort (to foil any rescue attempts) and were allowed to carry their own nooses, which I am sure cheered them up no end. Crach was to be hanged by his own kinsmen, his uncle and cousin. This was common practice. If it wasn't done properly, they would be hanged too.

The gallows was a simple structure, with just two uprights and a cross beam. Under the direction of the lord's steward, John de Baggeham, William was hanged first by being pushed off a ladder. But they didn't do anything quite as sophisticated for Trahaearn ap Hywel. They threw a rope over the cross beam and hauled him up. He was a big man and inconsiderately struggled, which eventually broke the cross beam.

It appears that they then hanged them both again from the uprights, though Trahaearn was already dead. William's rope broke a second time but they were sure he was dead. His face was black, his eyes were outside his eyelids, and the sockets were full of blood – along with his mouth, nostrils and ears. His tongue was black, inflamed and protruding. He could not have breathed. He remained hanging long enough for people to believe he was dead. They knew he was dead because he had released the contents of his bladder and bowels, which was always regarded as a sign apparently.

A report was made to de Breos that the gallows had collapsed but both men had died. The bodies were taken back to the town, to the house of Thomas Mathews, near St Mary's Church, and visitors came to see how justice had been done. Lady Mary and her servants

De Breos glanced up from his dinner briefly, looked out of the window, and was pleased with his work. (Original drawing by Ditta Szalkai)

York, where Rhys ap Maredudd was hanged, drawn and quartered. (LC-DIG-ppmsc-09035)

apparently prayed to Thomas de Cantilupe to intercede with God and restore William's life.

Thomas de Cantilupe, the former Bishop of Hereford, had died in 1282. However, there was a growing belief that he possessed magical powers. A bit of a long shot, you might think. But by midnight William showed signs of life. He started to breathe and moved his leg. He couldn't see and he couldn't speak. He could not swallow either, which isn't a surprise, and was fed on broth. Within a fortnight he had largely recovered. And, of course, the law said he could not be taken back for another turn on the gallows – though, when he was later questioned, he was terrified that they might try.

Now the big issue here was whether Crach represented a miracle. There had to be an enquiry. All these details, which open such a fascinating window into this largely obscure period of our history, come from the ecclesiastical enquiries into Thomas de Cantilupe and his possible canonisation. There were thirty-eight miracles associated with him, of which William the Scabby's story was the most compelling. All witnesses were questioned, including William himself, and everything was very carefully recorded.

The fact that he had confessed all his sins to a priest, had showed remorse, and prayed mightily, was very helpful. William always told anyone who would listen that on his way to the gallows he had prayed to God to be spared such a shameful death, for the sake of Sir Thomas. All he could remember of the execution was that the bishop had appeared before him and supported his feet. Later on, the bishop in white had come back and shoved his tongue back into his mouth.

Within a month Crach made a pilgrimage to Hereford, walking barefoot to give thanks at the tomb of Thomas de Cantilupe, his new best friend. He wore the noose around his neck, which he left at the tomb, along with a wax model of a gallows with a figure of a man hanging from it. He lived for about another ten years.

Sir Thomas had a lot to thank William for. After a long investigation, lasting thirteen years, he was made a saint in 1320. They decided that it was a miracle, pure and simple. There was no trickery or spells or superstition involved. William might just as well have thanked St Ethelbert, another popular contemporary sponsor of miracles in Hereford, and a man reputed to have spoken after his own beheading – a trick few others have since mastered. William the Scabby, however, was not keen to give it a try himself, despite his previous successes.

FAMILY TENSION

THE DE BREOS family maintained their position through military strength. They sold land that didn't belong to them, like Trewyddfa (Morriston). Their tenants were over-taxed and constantly fined. Eventually, the people took their grievances against William de Breos to the King's County Court in Carmarthen in 1299 and, on four separate occasions, he was summoned to Parliament to answer for his alleged misconduct. But it was his stepmother Mary who finally did for him when she got him into court over a debt of 800 marks. When the judge announced in favour of Mary, William, a man used to getting his own way, 'spoke coarse and contemptuous words' to the judge. As a result, he was thrown into the Tower for a while.

He continued to sell land that wasn't his. In fact, his gift of Gower to Edward II's unpopular favourite, Hugh Despenser, was part of the circumstances that led to civil war. The rebel barons attacked Gower and captured William's steward, who was decapitated by a baker in Swansea. When William himself died in 1326, Swansea passed into the ownership of a series of absentee managers.

Even 250 years after the Normans' arrival in Swansea, the two communities of English and Welsh continued to mistrust each other. In the Charter of 1306, no burgesses from the town could be indicted by a Welshman for any offences committed in the borough. The resentment of people whose homeland was occupied continued unchecked.

But there were inevitable changes. The Normans lost their language and their own identity. The Welsh started to use English money and English names. English people started to buy land in the Welsh area. In 1319, for example, Gillete and Agnes bought 'land and meadow' in Enesketti (Sketty), which was largely a Welsh area.

One of the consequences of the Black Death – which devastated the population in 1349, 1361 and 1369 – was that the distinction between Welsh and English eroded. All are equal in death, and the disease created opportunities for the living, no matter who they were.

'Hand it over. You can't hit him. He is not your son.'
(Author's collection)

AD 1326

EDWARD II

A King and his Stuff

GOWER HAD BEEN presented to Edward II's favourite Hugh Despenser, so when the King's wife Isabella – known to her friends as 'The She-Wolf of France' (her enemies were less polite) – rose in rebellion against him, he fled to South Wales in October 1326, clearly believing this would be the place to seek sanctuary.

He tried to gather an army to confront her, which does suggest that this was a bit more than a tiff or a spat for the couple. However, he could find little support and desperately looked for somewhere to hide. He eventually reached Neath with his royal treasure and sent messages ahead to Swansea to have the castle prepared for his arrival. He authorised an upgrade of its defences, realising that it was in poor condition. However, with support ebbing away, he had to turn back and was detained either just outside Neath or near Tonyrefail, depending on which version you believe. He was forced to abdicate and was either smothered or strangled in 1327. The commonly held story that he had an intimate encounter with a red-hot poker is probably a myth. But there is also a suggestion that he might have escaped and died, much later, in a monastery in Italy. No one can be sure.

But before he turned back, he sent much of his treasure on to Swansea. This was a mistake, as his successor, Edward III, was to discover when he tried to find it all. The treasure seemed to have disappeared, stolen (according to the Close Rolls of 1331) by some 'malefactors at Swayneseye'. To be honest, it was silly to expect anything different.

Most of the people of the town appear to have been implicated in some way or other, since the arrival of the King's treasure – without a

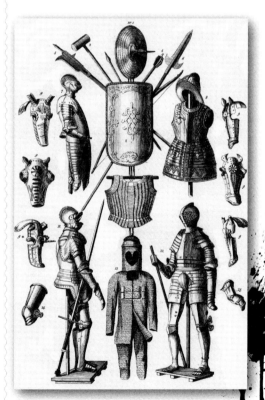

Within twenty-four hours the people of Swansea had got a brochure out into the neighbouring towns and villages, with price list and order form. (www. fromoldbooks.org)

proper guard – does not happen too often. Soon there were locals who were in possession of a full suit of armour, propped up in the corner of their cottage, with little idea what to do with it. Others had swords, the sort of posh clothing which even today would be out of place in Castle Gardens, boots and saddles. Three 'capellae de visura, with their appendages' had been spirited away too, and who indeed could be surprised?

One man had taken two horses, but he sent one back (presumably it was lame). In total the treasure was worth £60,000, which was an enormous sum. When Edward III finally got around to establishing a commission of enquiry to find out where his dad's money was, he was disappointed to find that it had all disappeared completely.

Coins from the treasure have been found in Neath and original documents have been found in the roof of a cottage in Gower, but most of it was never seen again. It might still be out there, somewhere. So if you come across a capellae de visura (with its appendages) you can have a decent guess where it came from.

THE WELSH ARE REVOLTING

GIVEN THE UNSTABLE conditions – plague, incompetence, corruption – it isn't surprising that there was a serious revolt in North Wales in 1400, when Owain Glyndwr declared himself Prince of Wales. The population seems to have been generally in favour of a Welsh revival and the insurrection became a national revolt. Armies marched backwards and forwards; there were skirmishes, battles and reprisals. The prospect of an independent Welsh nation encouraged Welsh soldiers to return home from England to join. Soldiers deserted the English army to fight with Glyndwr. The rebellion seemed to fulfil the predictions of Merlin.

Swansea Castle was desperately repaired, since in 1400 it was largely a ruin. The previous year, Richard II had stayed there on his way to Ireland and conditions were such that it set the standard for a number of Swansea guesthouses for centuries to come. A courtier complained that it was 'totally unfurnished and Richard had to sleep on straw during his sojourn'.

So they cleared out the ditches, men-at-arms were hired, and new locks were fitted to the doors of the gaol. They put fences around the lord's meadow in Morfa and brought in firewood to keep the accountants and stewards warm.

In 1403 the rebellion reached the south. By July, Glyndwr had taken and burnt Carmarthen. Other castles, like Llandeilo, Dynevor and Weobley, were taken. Swansea held out for a while. In September, ship-owners were commissioned to deliver supplies to the garrison. A merchant called Peter Courtenay was commissioned to deliver wheat, wine, ale, fish and oats. But Glyndwr marched through South Wales with a small number of French troops, bypassed Swansea altogether and headed for Cardiff. There was nothing to delay him; his supporters had already destroyed the castle. But really Swansea was never at the heart of the rebellion. And perhaps Swansea owes a huge favour to an old gentleman from Ynystawe, as we will see later.

Eventually, the rebellion fizzled out and Glyndwr disappeared and lived in disguise, perhaps in Herefordshire. The division between the English and the Welsh continued to blur, but it was still there in the attitudes towards authority that some of the locals displayed. Parts of the town were much more Welsh than others and remained so. In the nineteenth century, the children attending Cwm School in Bonymaen were still Welsh-speaking when children in other parts of the town were not. This, of course, was in Kilvey, which had always been separated from the town by the river.

One of the consequences of the rebellion is that the castle never really recovered. The land upon which it stood was regarded as having no value at all. By 1425 it no longer had a military function, and housed administrators. Its decline into a scenic ruin was now inevitable. It wasn't needed any more.

AD 1403

HOPCYN AP TOMOS

Man of the Year

THERE ARE THOSE amongst you who might consider it an indignity that the family home of one of Wales' finest literary figures has now become a caravan park. Hopcyn ap Tomos of Ynystawe, who was born in 1330, was a collector of Welsh literature; he arranged for text to be copied into what became known as *The Red Book of Hergest*, a collection of poems and stories, histories and herbal remedies. This remains one of the most important texts surviving from medieval Wales. Hopcyn was a great patron of the arts – supporting, amongst others, Casnodyn, the bard from Kilvey, who was famous across the whole of Wales. Fourteen of his compositions survive, which by all accounts went down a storm everywhere.

Hopcyn was regarded as a cultured man of wisdom and was also an authority on bardic prophecy. As a result, in July 1403 he was summoned to Carmarthen by Owain Glyndwr to prophesy what might happen to him. These were heady times, with the prophesies of Merlin – that the Welsh would rise and throw off the invader – apparently within grasp.

Glyndwr was not sure what he should do. He had choices, which did not sit comfortably with his military mind. Should he attack

In Ynystawe Park. (Author's collection)

Owain Glyndwr. (Courtesy of Seth Whales)

Pembroke? Or Swansea and then Cardiff? Or would he be better off advancing on Kidwelly? Tough decisions.

Now, it is always tricky predicting the future for a man who has a large and over-excitable army looking for recreational opportunities. What exactly can you predict? That one day he will meet someone who has a bigger and even more excitable army than his own, who will want to thread his liver on a stick and wave it from the battlements? Or do you tell the man who invited you what he wants to hear? It is a tough call.

Hopcyn's prophecy was suitably vague. Obviously, the more difficult the predictions are to interpret, the more accurate they will be. First of all, the prophet must make the subject feel clever by allowing them to think that only the gifted (like themselves) are capable of understanding the future. It also means that they will make themselves look stupid if they later claim that the prophet didn't know what they were saying and got it all wrong. It is a tricky game to play, but in such circumstances Hopcyn didn't have much choice. What he did, though, was a masterstroke.

Glyndwr interpreted Hopcyn's prophecy as indicating that he would be captured under a black banner somewhere between Carmarthen and Gower. Taking everything into consideration, Glyndwr decided that it would be best all round if he attacked Kidwelly and avoided The Black Banner of Destiny.

The consequences were clear for all to see. Glyndwr succeeded in his assault on Kidwelly and could not be apprehended on the road to Gower because he didn't use it. But most importantly of all, neither Glyndwr nor his large and unsophisticated army ever went near the family home of Hopcyn ap Tomos in Ynystawe. You have got to hand it to him, truly a master at work.

There is a fine memorial to him in Ynystawe Park. It was erected originally in 1959 but sadly became rather overlooked. Thankfully, it has recently been restored. His memory is preserved. And, as we have seen before, the past still exists in our unsuspecting lives today; his mother and eldest daughter were both called Tanglwst, and the bridge across the river beyond the park is called Ynystanglws Bridge.

AD 1500s

SWANSEA IN ELIZABETHAN TIMES

SWANSEA WAS FAR away from the centre of influence and power. Ordinary life went on as it had done since the Welsh insurrections ended. The town was noisy and dirty, with muddy streets decorated with filth and dung; a smelly breeding ground for disease. Pot holes and ruts would fill with water and other unspeakable matter. The town authorities were keen to pave as many of the streets as they could afford. They would also pay people to clean the streets. Corporation records show that Ales Lovid, for example, was paid to clean 'the market and lane to Wind Street'. Ales, where are you when we need you still?

They were keen to preserve the quality of the water supply. After all, the river down on the Strand was tidal and brackish, and the ditches and streams around the town were merely open sewers. You can understand their anxiety. Clothes were washed and animals skinned and prepared next to (or indeed sometimes inside) the town well. This was eventually prohibited in 1553. But if you were sensible you drank either wine or beer. They were safer.

Everything was thrown in the street – general waste, animal waste, human waste. Rats and other vermin found plenty to entertain them. They were always a threat to food stores and to livestock. Every town, including Swansea, had to have a net with which to catch crows. Rewards were offered to anyone presenting the heads of crows, magpies or rooks – a penny for three heads. Six unbroken eggs got you a penny too. Twelve starlings' heads earned you a penny. Killing a badger was worth 12d, which probably transformed the financial position of Richard Johns in 1598. His friend Morgan David did even better. He was given 4d for a wild cat and 16d for two foxes. Obviously this was the perfect situation for a boy with a catapult.

There were two popular forms of entertainment for the townspeople when they had tired of chasing birds – bull baiting and cock fighting. It is hard to believe, but no butcher could kill a bull which had not been baited by dogs or he would have to face a fine based upon the size of the animal. They believed that the baiting actually improved the quality of the meat.

As you might expect in a busy port, where a living was to be made in that interesting space between buying and selling, customs officials were not very popular. In 1575, John Myddleton, on duty in the customs house in Swansea, was attacked by four men. He was wounded in the head with a dagger. Bones were 'taken out of his said head whereof long time after he languished and lay at the point of death'. You can hardly blame him. (Court of Star Chamber)

> The French tried to establish a colony in Florida, but in 1565 they were driven out by the Spanish. They fled across the Atlantic and eventually landed in Swansea, where the people did what they could to 'succour the poor sea-worn fugitives with the horrors of a fiendish slaughter among the lagoons and sand dunes of Florida still fresh in their minds'. I understand that holiday charter flights land in Cardiff in much the same state today.

Cock fighting usually saw two birds with sharpened beak and claw paired against each other. On other occasions, anything up to twenty birds could be put into the ring and spectators would bet on the last one standing. You can see a fine example of a cock pit in the St Fagan's folk museum in Cardiff, which gives you some idea of the intensity of such an occasion.

The citizens also looked forward to the occasional appearance of travelling theatre

Ales and the Street Cleaning Band. (By kind permission of the Thomas Fisher Rare Book Library, University of Toronto)

companies, who would appear in the Town Hall. We know this because there still survive bills which were presented to the performers for windows broken during performances. Someone was over-excited, but whether it was the actors or the audience sadly isn't recorded.

People went bowling on the greens and the better-off played real tennis, which was an indoor game. The most popular pastimes were also indoor entertainment – cards and dice. And, of course, these gambling games frequently caused 'anger and cursing, debility and killing and fighting among men', as a contemporary source has suggested.

Court records show that Hopkyn Vaughan claimed he was assaulted during a card game in the kitchen of Rosser Vaughan's house in Llansamlet. Whatever caused the dispute, it gathered some momentum because Hopkyn later claimed that he was assaulted a second time in St Mary's Street. Rosser couldn't have done it, he said, since he was bowling at the time down on the Burrows. Strange to think that, just like today, disputes starting in Llansamlet will re-emerge in the town centre.

'It is called style. You wouldn't understand.' (By kind permission of the Thomas Fisher Rare Book Library, University of Toronto)

AD 1557

A STONE'S THROW FROM OXWICH

IT ALL STARTED on Boxing Day 1557. There was a savage westerly gale and a French vessel carrying wool, almonds, figs and raisins was wrecked on the Gower coast. Who cared if it was late? This was an excellent Christmas present – they were already halfway to a decent pudding. Members of the Mansel family from Llanddewi, led by Sir Rice Mansel, were first to the ship and carried off as much as they could to their houses in Oxwich. Survivors of the wreck were taken prisoner.

However, the law said that the rights to any wreck belonged to Sir George Herbert over in Swansea. He sent his representatives to recover the booty but, since there was no warrant, the people of Oxwich bought time by refusing to hand it over. When he found out about it, Sir George rushed to Gower. He was a man who didn't like having his privileges eroded, especially by a family of villains like the Mansels – and who can blame him?

His men headed to the brand-new designer property, otherwise known as Oxwich Castle, to recover what was his by right. They marched through the village, breaking into houses at random to recover the booty and take it to the church for storage. They called at the parsonage to see Richard Cosin, the parson, and burst

'So here it is, Merry Christmas, everybody's having fun ...'

The gate at Oxwich Castle. (Author's collection)

into his bedchamber to seize his share. He was not alone, and witnesses later suggested that the relationship between the woman guest and the parson was a little more familiar than they might have anticipated.

Then they marched on the castle where they were met at the gate by a son of the family, Edward Mansel, who, after looking for help, had returned with his aunt, Anne. Words were exchanged. Anne had earlier met Sir George on the road and warned him not to 'contend for such pylfery goods'. But that is exactly what he intended to do. As far as he was concerned, the goods were his, so he and his men stormed the castle.

The gate was defended and 'Old Mistress Mansel' placed her horse in the gateway as an obstruction. Edward advanced and hit Sir George with his stick, which even then was not universally regarded as the best way of calming a situation. Anne tried her best to push her nephew back through the gate, urging him to get in. But Edward was not ready to listen. He drew his sword and pushed past her, ready for action.

'How now are ye come hither to rob and invade me?'

Sir George looked at him and said that he would truss him up and 'send him to his father like a cocke'. There was a bit of a scuffle and one of Sir George's men, Watkin John ap Watkin, picked up a stone and hurled it at Edward.

He missed. The stone struck Anne Mansel in the middle of her forehead. She died instantly. Those defending the gate started to shout, 'Murder! Murder!' and the assailants withdrew.

The inquest later found that the wound was 'of the breadth of two thumbs and the depth even to the brain, though the stone was of no great bigness'.

The case was taken to the Star Chamber in London, and the verbatim records of witnesses' testimonies that you can read here are a wonderful window to the past. And of course, you can't throw stones at old ladies, not even for a bag of almonds. Sir George Herbert was heavily fined by the Crown after being found guilty of wrongfully entering premises; he had to pay damages to the Mansels and return all the goods taken in the raid on Oxwich. Watkin John ap Watkin was pardoned. And George never got his raisins back.

39

AD 1607

THE GREAT DELUGE

I **THINK THERE HAVE** been three turning points in Swansea's history – the arrival of the Normans, the arrival of industry and the arrival of German bombers. But there may have been a fourth. And if that really did happen, it was perhaps the greatest turning point of them all, for there is evidence that our coastline was reshaped forever by a tsunami.

Let us start with the things that we do know. We know that the whole of the Bristol Channel experienced an enormous surge of water in 1607. Some sources suggest that it happened in 1606, but that reflects the fact that the year changed officially in March. The flood was called 'The Great Deluge' and was described in a contemporary broadsheet as 'God's warning to his people of England'. The idea that they were being punished appealed very much to the

contemporary mind. Pamphlets like 'Woefull Newes from Wales' were sold in London, giving those not involved a vicarious thrill at the thought of the sinful nature of those who lived along the Bristol Channel.

It began at about 9 a.m. on Tuesday 20 January, and the morning was cold but bright. This is a significant detail. If it had been grey and stormy then the deluge could have been a 'storm surge', like the one which devastated the Norfolk Broads in the twentieth century. Some believe that there was a severe depression off the southern coast of Ireland and that the event was preceded by strong winds. But if it came out of a clear blue sky, as others believe, then something under the water caused it. Certainly, some accounts suggest that the sea was 'driven back before the wave came', a classic indication of a tidal wave.

There could have been a landslide off the continental shelf between Ireland and Cornwall, or an earthquake along an active fault system in the sea south of Ireland. Or indeed both, with one causing the other. If you had been caught by it, however, the reasons wouldn't have troubled you greatly as you desperately tried to run away from an inexorable wall of water.

As the water came up the Channel it would have been squeezed by the shoreline, which would have increased its height and velocity. Around Swansea it has been estimated that the water was travelling at about 30mph at a height of 18ft. It probably penetrated 2 miles

Once, much of this was farmland. (Author's collection)

(Original drawing by Ditta Szalkai)

inland. By the time it reached Monmouth it was possibly 25ft high and travelling at 38mph. It seems to have reached as far as Glastonbury. Whatever the cause, it has been called Britain's worst natural disaster.

Hundreds of acres on both sides of the Bristol Channel were inundated – and to a remarkable depth too. There are churches which still carry upon them the level that the water reached. You can see an inscription on the wall of St Bride's Church at Wentloog Level, showing the height of the water at 5ft 6in. In some places, churches were swamped entirely so that only the tips of the steeples reached above the water. St Mary's Church in Cardiff was entirely washed away. It was a truly cataclysmic event. The waves washed in at an astonishing speed – 'no greyhound would have escaped by running before them'. The waves appeared as 'mighty hilles of water tombling over one another in such sort as if the greatest mountains in the world had overwhelmed the lowe villages or marshy grounds'.

Over 500 people were said to have drowned in South Wales alone. Overall, it is thought that more than 2,000 were 'devoured by these outrageous waters'. In Swansea, 'a great many harms were done'. Strangely, there is no mention of the event at all in the Corporation records. However, there is a request for assistance from Aberavon, which 'hath sustained grett lostes and hindrances upon theyer seae walles'. Swansea generously 'thought good in charity to bestowe the some of xx.s as theyr ffree gyft and benevolence to the forseid distressed inhabytance of Aven'. Twenty shillings. How generous. And if the water devastated Aberavon, Cardiff, Somerset and Gloucestershire, then it is hard to believe that Swansea escaped unscathed.

However, there is well-documented evidence that farmland and woodland disappeared under the sea. The coast along Swansea Bay is believed to have curved around further out to sea than it does now, from Mumbles Head to Margam Wood. There is evidence of a bridle path leading from Penrice Castle to Margam Abbey, passing some way out past Mumbles Head.

In the Great Deluge, farmland called the Green Grounds (in the bay beyond the lighthouse) was swamped. There is talk of a farmhouse and meadows. Certainly in 1899 W. Llewellyn Morgan, in his *Antiquarian Survey of East Gower*, wrote that, 'A slab of rock was dragged up on the Green Grounds in 1885 bearing marks of a chisel and cement. It is supposed to have come from the old house of the Angels said to have existed on these lands.'

The Angels were important landowners in the Mumbles area and tradition suggests that they owned large stretches of land, which were then submerged. In 1818, the family claimed in court that they had land before 'the sea had made its inroads on that flat which now forms the admired bay of Swansea'.

So perhaps the bay that we know so well was in fact shaped by a tsunami 400 years ago. Or by a storm surge. And however nature did it, nature of course could do it again at any time …

AD 1643

THE CIVIL WAR

A Smile, a Song and a Horse Supper

JUST AS WE saw in the Welsh rebellion of Owain Glyndwr, Swansea was a long way from any big Civil War action. Obviously the town had Royalist sympathies, because the absent lord of the town was the Earl of Worcester, who was very much a King's man. Not only that, but in general the upper classes and the very poorest supported the Royalist cause. The Parliamentarians were supported by the middle classes. Since there were precious few of those in Swansea, it was largely a Royalist town. In addition, little had been done to translate political pamphlets into Welsh, and much of what happened to fuel the Civil War happened through the press.

The Earl turned up in the town in 1643 – an unusual occurrence, probably to encourage support for the King. They even spent £10 on horse meat for a celebratory dinner. Quite a party I'd say, especially when you consider that

Swansea Castle today. (Author's collection)

he spent 16s repairing the turret of the castle. Now you might not think that this was a great sum, but when Oliver Cromwell later surveyed Gower in 1650, the 'ancient decayed building called the New Castle' was valued by his agents at £2 10s. Obviously a property with potential for the imaginative developer – but there was no interest. What we can see today is largely what they did then, when it was 'disgarrisoned and its works slighted'.

Swansea had some minor strategic importance. It had a castle (of sorts), a garrison, and was a port of entry for the import of arms. In fact, an agreement was made in July 1643 with a couple of Frenchmen to import muskets and gunpowder. This was a risky enterprise since the navy was in the hands of the Parliamentarians, but once the transaction was successfully completed many of the muskets were found to be faulty.

The campaign flowed backwards and forwards across west Wales. Sometimes it was

'Remind me dear. Which side are we on today?'
(Author's collection)

the Royalists in charge. Sometimes it wasn't. The town, like most of Wales, provided troops for the Royalist army. The problem in Swansea was that they could only find forty fit men. Perhaps it was ever thus.

The town also provided money through a tax levied on coal exports, which was greater than the price of the coal itself.

The property of Parliamentarians was seized, but if they adopted the Royalist cause then it was all returned. Men changed sides for their own survival and profit. Like traders everywhere, the merchants of Swansea didn't much care who was in charge as long as they were left alone to get on with their lives. And really, the differences between the two sides were not particularly local issues. The motivating passions were not strongly felt; it was all happening a long way away.

But there was one significant difference between the two sides. When Parliamentary forces entered Swansea under General Laugharne, such was their delight that they spent over £1 on 'wine and beer for entertainment'. Their catering budget couldn't stretch to a horse supper.

Oliver Cromwell.

AD 1760

ON THE ROCKS

The Wreck of the *Caesar*

THIS IS A tragic story from a treacherous coastline. If you stand on the cliffs and look down into the bracken, you can see the evidence of this disaster: a group of stones which make up a rough circle. It could never be a natural phenomenon. Someone put them there deliberately. And they did so to mark a grave, a mass grave, away from the rocks which mark the shoreline. For this is the hidden secret of Pwlldu, where the bracken won't grow.

The story starts with the Press Gang, feared and hated everywhere. Their job was to find men to serve in the navy, by whatever means they could. This generally meant kidnap and they scoured coastal communities in times of

'Oh hear us when we cry to thee, for those in peril on the sea.'

need, snatching men at random. They would be shoved into the hold of some leaking tub, sometimes handcuffed, and taken away without a chance to tell anyone. When it was known that the Press Gang were operating, the men of Pennard, for example, would hide as far away as they could until they had gone.

It was November 1760 and the Press Gang left their usual haunts. Pickings were thin. The Ship Inn, the Beehive and the Plume of Feathers were not proving profitable, so they went off to Mumbles where they met a group of local men returning home to Gower. It was the opportunity they had been looking for. The local men, however, vigorously resisted their advances and there was a fight – during which John Voss of Nicholaston was attacked with a cutlass. His arm was almost severed. Others joined in and the Press Gang were driven away. Voss was taken to Swansea to be treated.

The Press Gang had come from a ship called the *Caesar* which was sailing from Bristol to Plymouth, harvesting men for the navy as it went. By the time it left Swansea on 28 November, it was carrying at least sixty-eight men squashed in the hold. However, the tide and the weather were against them and the ship turned back towards Mumbles.

Visibility was poor and they mistook Pwlldu Head for Mumbles. Confused and disorientated, the *Caesar* ran aground between vicious rocks. The sides of the ship were soon torn out. A few officers and crew escaped onto the rocks and up the cliffs, but everyone else was trapped in the hold. The officers made their way up to Pennard to find out where they were, but never mentioned their human cargo back on the ship.

When the locals arrived at the rocks the next morning, the sea was full of wreckage and battered bodies. The pressed men had been left in the hold, many of them handcuffed, and they had drowned in the rising tide. John Voss was there amongst the onlookers and he saw the officer who had previously attacked him. Now he was dead, draped in seaweed. The ship's cargo of munitions – muskets, pistols, swords – was washed up for months afterwards.

The captain of the *Caesar*, Adam Drake, said that at least sixty-five men and three women had been lost. The people of Pennard said they found ninety-seven bodies. The villagers buried them in a communal grave at a point where there was sufficient soil, beyond the reach of the high tide. The grave was marked with the circle of rocks that you can still see. The site is called Graves End and is marked as such on maps. The site where the ship ran aground is called Caesar's Hole.

It is a sad and inaccessible place, rarely visited or acknowledged. But when you are there you can understand why some consider it haunted still.

Left *'Please Captain. Can't we take the girl instead? Just this once?'* (Author's collection)

Below *Gravesend at Pwlldu.* (Author's collection)

AD 1786

SMUGGLERS' TALES

IN ITS TIME, smuggling bound together the community along the shoreline. The advantages for smugglers were obvious. Contraband could easily be brought ashore unobserved and Swansea itself provided an easy and accessible market. Secluded wooded valleys provided the perfect cover; one of the tracks leading along the Bishopston Valley is still called Smuggler's Lane. Pwlldu in Gower was reputedly used more than any other beach in the whole of the Bristol Channel. The house that you can see there was once the Beaufort Inn, and the landlord there allowed smugglers to use his cellars for storage.

The customs man was the villain; the smuggler was a working-class hero, rather like the poacher. He seemed to confront an unfeeling and distant authority and stand up for the ordinary man. Whole communities were implicated; smuggling was an essential part of the fabric of their lives. In stories, the customs man was always outwitted by local knowledge

and spirit. There are stories of kegs of brandy hidden inside the altar in Port Eynon, and of pitched battles on Rhossili beach.

The kings of the local smugglers in the late eighteenth century were the notorious Arthur gang, who operated from their farms, the Great Highway and the Little Highway in Pennard. William Arthur was regarded as the most daring of all smugglers and ran a well-resourced operation. In 1786 there was a raid on Great Highway by twelve customs men – but Arthur had been kept well informed and they were confronted by over 100 locals, many of whom Arthur employed. The customs officials were driven away.

The Arthurs covered most of the coast and had an extensive workforce who earned more than an agricultural worker ever could. The gang were seen as benevolent employers, which didn't do the local economy many favours. For a short period smuggling was a key industry and a major employer in the area.

Swansea in the eighteenth century. (Author's collection)

GOOD FORTUNE

In 1626 *The Fortune* from Hamburg, laden with lots of exciting goods, was driven by the winds into Swansea Harbour. It wasn't really a problem. The captain and his men went ashore and into the town; the unexpected and welcome bonus of rest and relaxation for sailors in troubled times beckoned. And I am quite sure they had a wonderful time. Except that when they went back to their ship it wasn't there. Today it happens to the Ford Mondeo you left just behind The Kingsway when you went for a curry. Then it was a 150-ton ship.

Eighteen local men, under the inspired leadership of Robert Daniel, had sailed it away. They went across the Channel to Barnstaple in Devon where they sold the entire cargo of lemons and oranges in the same way that a man in a pub today will try to sell you a DVD player. Times change, but dodgy deals stay the same.

There was healthy profit to be made in the considerable gap between buying and selling. Tea, for example, was 7*d* per lb in Holland. But it sold in Britain, after duty, at 4*s*. With that sort of price differential, everyone could be a winner – except the customs man. Men would be paid to do the heavy lifting – a cargo of eighty casks of brandy would require forty men, who carried two each, slung by ropes over back and chest. Why work on the farm for a week when you could earn more in two nights?

Myths about smuggling became part of the folk memory. Consider the keg of brandy seized in Great Highway. It was placed in the kitchen and guarded by a lone excise man who sent for help. William Arthur, they say, went into the cellar below the kitchen and bored a hole through the floorboards into the keg. Thus it was drained and the contents quietly taken away. So, when the reinforcements arrived, all they found was a colleague guarding an empty barrel. A good story certainly, though the same story is told in a variety of other places, like Polperro.

The community was always stronger than the handful of officials. In 1804, when the business was raided, much of the local area was implicated. The excise men could not confront the crowd that gathered when they turned up to seize the goods. In fact, they had to release some of what they had seized to guarantee their own safety. People turned up with quills that they used like straws to suck up the brandy from the kegs. The guards themselves couldn't be trusted either. In the end their captain allowed them to drink from the kegs too, since he was unable to stop them.

But of course it couldn't go on. The development of the coastguard and the virtual blockade of the English Channel by the navy brought the golden days of smuggling to an end in the early nineteenth century. So William Arthur put his considerable business skills to more legitimate use. He became a mine and canal owner.

Barrels laid out along the shoreline. (Denise Hunter)

AD 1816

FANNY IMLAY

Keeping it in the Family

POOR FANNY IMLAY. She died in the Mackworth Arms in Swansea, on 9 October 1816, at just twenty-two years old. She lived her life in the wrong place, at the wrong time and with the wrong people. What was missing in her complicated home was happiness. Sometimes the ordinary is enough.

She was born in Le Havre during the French Revolution, the illegitimate daughter of the British feminist Mary Wollstonecraft and the American businessman Gilbert Imlay. When the relationship failed, Mary tried to kill herself on two occasions – once taking an overdose of laudanum and once jumping off Putney Bridge.

Mary then married William Godwin but died in childbirth from a retained placenta. The child was a girl who was also called Mary. Fanny and Mary were brought up by Godwin and his new wife. Thus Fanny was living with people who were neither her father nor her mother, and with a half-sister who had killed her mother.

Eventually, into all this emotional soup walked the poet Percy Shelley. He visited Godwin and, whilst Fanny may have fallen in love with him, it was with the younger Mary that Shelley had an affair. Together they disappeared to Europe for a while. Mary wrote *Frankenstein* and her sister Claire had an affair with Lord Byron. It was such a tangled web.

Mary Wollstonecraft threw herself from Putney Bridge. (Author's collection)

Fanny left London for Bristol in October 1816 and moved on then to Swansea. Perhaps she went to Swansea with the intention of visiting her grandfather, who was living on a farm at Laugharne. Perhaps on her way she stopped off in Bath to see Shelley and Mary, who had moved there a couple of months earlier. No one can be quite sure.

Fanny was found dead in her room.
(Author's collection)

She arrived at the Mackworth Arms (now demolished) where the coaches terminated on the east side of Wind Street. The *Cambrian* newspaper tried to outline what happened, describing her as a 'respectable looking female ... from Bristol. She took tea and retired to rest, telling the chambermaid she was exceedingly fatigued and would take care of the candle herself.' When she didn't appear at breakfast, they forced the door open. She was found with the remains of a bottle of laudanum on the table and a note:

I have long determined that the best thing I could do was to put an end to the existence of a being whose birth was unfortunate ...

Apparently, the name was torn off and had been burnt. Her suicide note was written in the spaces around a letter from her stepfather to Shelley.

The reasons for her suicide can never be known. Perhaps life was too complicated. Perhaps life without Shelley was impossible for her. She had already sent letters to Mary and to her stepfather which had alarmed them to such an extent that they had both set off after her, but it was too late. Shelley stayed in Swansea to deal with the consequences. There are stories that Shelley tore her name from the suicide note to conceal her identity, but that can't be proved. At the inquest she was declared dead, rather than a suicide. Shelley did not claim her body and thus she was buried in a paupers' grave in St John's Church (now St Matthew's) near High Street station.

The family said she had gone to Ireland. Indeed, it was a long time before some family members discovered she was dead. Then they claimed that she had died of a cold in Wales. When they admitted suicide, they said it was because Shelley loved Mary, not her.

Godwin wrote to his daughter Mary: 'Go not to Swansea: disturb not the silent dead: do nothing to destroy the obscurity she so much desired.'

Perhaps it is appropriate that there is no known image of poor Fanny Imlay.

When Shelley spoke of it to Byron, he said he felt more anguish over her death than he did over the suicide of his wife Harriet two months later.

AD 1838–1858

THE STRANGE STORY OF BARON SPOLASCO

YOU MAY NOT have heard about Baron Spolasco. And when you have, you might wonder why he is remembered on a fresco on Patagonia Walk in the Marina.

Who he was is not easy to answer. But what he was is very simple. He was a charlatan, a confidence trickster, but most of all a quack doctor. He knew that treatments were often based upon faith; patients wanted to believe that a doctor had access to secrets which were denied to them. Spolasco exploited such trust. He saw desperate people in pain, who clutched at the hope he offered. He took their money and offered them worthless medication and sometimes they died. Because Spolasco was hollow, everything he did was built on sand. He was a chancer. And he took chances with other people's lives.

An apparently tragic incident became his great opportunity. On 19 January 1838, the steamer *Killarney* from Cork to Bristol, carrying thirty-seven people and 600 pigs, ran aground in a storm. The pigs were taken away by locals when they were washed up on the shore and twenty-one survivors were left clinging to a rock in Renney Bay. During the rescue, Spolasco said that his eight-year-old son had been drowned. Who can say? In the reports of the wreck, he appears to be called Count Smolensky and the tragedy of the death of his son, if indeed it was ever the truth, is merely another aspect of his tireless self-promotion. He wrote a popular book about his survival and the death of a son who may never have existed.

Of course, the truth of the matter was that he had been run out of Cork, where it seems he practised as a doctor – and practise, of course, is a word with alternative meanings. There were people after him. His real name was probably John Williams and he came from the north of England, possibly Leeds. But the truth became lost. His whole life appears to have been a tissue of lies. All his energies went into creating his own myth. He said that he was 'consulted in cases of difficulty and danger by physicians and surgeons in all parts of the world ... relative to

> *" Qui N' A. Sante N' A. Rien."*
>
> **MOST IMPORTANT TO THE AFFLICTED!!!**
>
> **T**HE Celebrated BARON SPOLASCO—the most successful Practioner of Medicine and Surgery in the World !!!—having been called professionally to Wales, may be consulted at his residence,
>
> **2, ADELAIDE-PLACE, SWANSEA,**
> relative to every Disease to which the human frame is liable.
>
> In consequence of the numerous Patients that daily crowd round Baron Spolasco's Consulting Rooms, he has been induced to prolong his stay in Swansea beyond the period which he originally designed. Those who require his advice would do well, therefore, to make immediate application, as they may not again have an opportunity afforded them of consulting so successful a Practitioner. It may be well to observe, that the Baron's stay in Swansea cannot be very protracted, seeing that he must return to his residence at Bristol, between which city and Bath, he purposes to spend the winter.—The *destitute* poor will receive advice *gratuitously*.
>
> 2, Adelaide Place, Oct. 18, 1838.
>
> Several very bad cases are under treatment ; and one is subj ined which has been successfully treated by the Baron within the last week, and reference to his Pamphlets is respectfully requested for further proofs of his successful practice.
>
> "I, CATHERINE SMITH, of the Rutland-Arms, Swansea, do certify, that I have suffered for a long period from a virulenty ulcerated leg, which considerably impaired my health, and that I consulted several Medical and Surgical Gentlemen in this town, but could get no relief, until I placed myself under the care of Baron Spolasco, who not only cured my leg in two dressings, but perfectly restored my health. I have just cause, indeed, to return God thanks for having sent this gentleman to Swansea, and I sincerely hope that other sufferers, such as I was, will apply to him, that they may derive similar benefit. My cure is indeed truly miraculous "CATHERINE SMITH."
>
> "Rutland-Arms, Swansea, Oct. 18, 1839."

(By kind permission of SWW Media)

all the diseases incidental to human nature'. He was like those who dress up in white and wander round hospital corridors pretending to be doctors.

He went initially to Bristol and then arrived in Swansea at the right time, just before industry destroyed any chance of the town becoming a holiday retreat for wealthy gentlefolk. Spolasco wrote his own publicity. Indeed, hardly a week went by without another eulogy to his skill as a scientific surgical operator or bone setter in the *Cambrian* newspaper. 'Any individual who has lost his or her nose can be supplied with a real one.' He claimed to cure gout, eruptions of the skin, impotency, hysterics, dysentery, corns – and generally all with the same pill.

Why would anyone believe him? Because they wanted to.

And, of course, Spolasco knew that the more someone paid, the more willing they were to believe that the cure had worked. What his patients wanted was confidence and belief, and so he became a parasite living on the vulnerable, challenged by neither proof nor evidence.

In Ireland he had been an expert in pretty much everything. In Swansea he appears to have concentrated on legs. In fact, he claimed that when his horse Scipio broke a leg whilst training for Swansea races, he successfully reset it.

He celebrated the first anniversary of his rescue by providing a whole roast ox for the poor, though of course these were not the people he was really interested in. He settled in Adelaide Street and received patients – including Susannah Thomas from Bridgend, who consulted him about abdominal pain. For 22s 6d he supplied two pills and powder, just as he did for all his patients. She took the prescription and died. An autopsy suggested that his wonder cure had hastened her death. He was accused of manslaughter but was acquitted.

In 1840 he was accused of forging government stamps to authenticate his pills. Whilst awaiting trial in prison (he was acquitted) he composed a ballad about himself and his genius, which is reproduced on the wall in the Marina.

In 1843 he found himself in trouble again, this time over the death of Revd Edward Matthew Davies of Park Place near Parkmill in Gower, who died of kidney disease. Davies had met Spolasco at a sale in Gower and was persuaded to call on him for a consultation. On arrival, Revd Davies had to hand over 5s as an 'entry fee'. Then he had to pay a guinea as a consultation fee. The treatment was going to cost twenty guineas. The reverend only had £12 so Spolasco magnanimously took that and handed over the medication. Revd Davies returned home, took to his bed, took part of the pill and part of the powder he had been prescribed, and died the following day. He was thirty-eight years old. The conclusion of the post-mortem was that the medication had not killed him. He had an abdominal tumour and dodgy kidneys. But the medication hadn't done anything to keep him alive either. The coroner commented on the morality of 'taking money from the pockets of a person labouring under a

The memorial is hidden away on Patagonia Walk, and perhaps it is just as well. (Author's collection)

deadly disease'. Sadly, the questionable actions of the Baron did not fall within his remit.

Revd Davies, it was decided, died 'by the visitation of God in a natural way'. He was buried in the beautiful churchyard at Ilston, where he rests somewhere beneath a weathered and forgotten stone, remembered not for what he did himself but for what someone else did to him. It isn't a fate you would wish on yourself.

Spolasco's reputation started to wane. Inevitably, perhaps, he was named in a paternity suit. He may have issued commemorative medals describing himself as The Real Friend of the Afflicted, but he was not a real friend to his child. In July 1848, he was arrested in Birmingham for his failure to pay maintenance for a child in Gloucester. During his appearance before the magistrates, he threatened to take legal action against anyone who called him John Williams, which we might consider significant. He maintained that his name was Baron John William Adolphus Augustus Frederick Spolasco. No one was inclined to believe him. After some discussion, and not a little theatrical display, the Baron finally consented to pay the arrears to the young woman.

He was picked up by the police a second time in July 1849, when he unwisely visited Gloucester. He seemed to have forgotten his little responsibility. He was forced to pay up once again.

Eventually, he moved on. First to London, where he accused a sixteen-year-old servant girl of taking a diamond ring from him. Her defence was that she had taken it in revenge after he had assaulted her. It isn't hard to decide who to believe. Then he went to New York. He might have arrived in full pomp but his fortunes declined and he died in 1858 from cancer, in poverty.

There were many decent people who suffered at his hands, prescribed worthless powders and false hope, and yet it is his deceit and avarice that are preserved on one of our walls for all to see. History can be a strange thing at times.

AD 1843

THE REBECCA RIOTS

THE REBECCA RIOTS were born out of rural desperation. The starting point was what was perceived as a tax on rural life through the tolls that were charged for moving along the roads. The state of the roads was especially poor. Tolls run by private trusts had been established to improve the standards of the thoroughfares by reinvesting income. But the trusts were profit-making. The roads did not seem to improve at all and the income the tolls generated seemed to disappear. Resentment grew. Adding to this was a build-up of fear and anger about a way of life coming to an end. Cheap food imports were destroying the domestic market. Rural livelihoods and families were at risk. The population had already started to drift towards the towns in search of work.

The movement started in Carmarthenshire. A man dressed as a woman acted as the 'Rebecca' and his followers – the Daughters of Rebecca – pulled down gates and smashed toll houses before disappearing into the night. However, Pontarddulais was the site of the only confrontation between Rebecca and the authorities.

Pontarddulais was enclosed by six toll gates, which effectively controlled all entry to the town. It was not a surprise that the wave of discontent washing across Wales should inspire a response in the Bont.

Troops had been sent to Wales to confront the insurrection and, on 22 June 1843, they marched through the Bont on their way to Carmarthen. Their passage was clearly an inspiration in Pontarddulais. On 6 July, the Bolgoed Gate, near the Fountain Inn, was attacked, with a local boy from Goppa, Daniel Lewis, dressed as Rebecca. The gate was destroyed – and when the constables arrived the next day, no one would say anything.

On 20 July the Rhydypandy Gate, on the mountain road from Morriston to Clydach, was attacked. The gate was destroyed and the board displaying tolls was smashed. Two days later, the Poundffald Gate in Three Crosses was pulled down. The owner was pelted with rocks and bits of broken gate by the jeering mob.

The whole area was in a volatile state. There was an air of disorder and intimidation, with men forced to take part and others just turning up for the entertainment. But the mood was changing, with the rioters becoming increasingly violent. The attack on the Ty Coch Gate in St Thomas was carried out by colliers, not by the farming community. The gate was cut down

Wynford Vaughan Thomas, writer and broadcaster, was a direct descendant of Daniel Lewis from Goppa.

At Hendy. Notice that the date is wrong. (Author's collection)

with saws and burnt in a lime kiln. The toll receiver, Margaret Arnold, recognised one of the rioters but she was struck with an iron bar. Swansea was already crawling with policemen. The 73rd and 75th Regiments of Foot, together with over 400 Light Dragoons, were in town – and yet forty rioters had destroyed the gate unopposed.

Something had to be done.

A reward for information was offered and had the desired effect, after a fashion anyway. John Jones from Llangyfelach went to the police in Swansea and gave them a list of six men who he said had led the attack on the Bolgoed Gate. The names included that of Daniel Lewis but generally featured the Morgan family, with whom he was involved in a dispute about grazing rights on Llangyfelach Common.

The arrests didn't go too well. They picked up Daniel Lewis – who was rather amused by the whole thing – but things got a bit trickier when they tried to deal with the Morgan family. They negotiated the torrent of abuse from one of the Morgan wives without too many problems and took her husband away. But when they turned up on a Sunday to arrest the father, William Morgan, in his farmhouse at Cwmcille Fach Farm in Felindre, things rather fell apart.

Inspector Rees was attacked by the mother and Captain Napier was thrown to the ground in the yard by her boys. In the struggle, he shot one of the Morgans in response to being attacked with a hammer. The Inspector narrowly avoided a pan of boiling water that was thrown at him. Police colleagues waiting at the end of the lane responded to the pistol shot and arrived to effect the arrest. The 73rd Regiment of Foot were sent to Felindre later in the day to arrest the remainder of the Morgan family. Not surprisingly, John Jones was forced to live in the police station for his own protection.

The unrest continued but the agenda shifted as a more violent and criminal element became involved. Inevitably, sympathy started to ebb. So when Jack Hughes of Tyisha near Tumble decided to lead an attack on the Hendy and Pontarddulais Gates, information was leaked to both Captain Napier in Swansea and Major Parlby in Carmarthen. They both turned up without informing the other, at the bottom of Pontarddulais, on the evening of 6 September 1843.

There were eight officers and three magistrates from Swansea watching the Pontarddulais Gate. Led by a Rebecca on a white horse, the insurgents came down from Fforest and started to demolish the gate and the gatehouse. Napier and his men confronted them. Rebecca immediately fired a pistol at Napier and missed. The police returned fire and the rioters fled, desperately trying to cross the bridge into Carmarthenshire where they thought they might be safe. Napier dragged Hughes from his horse but was then hit from behind. He was saved by his officers, who shattered Hughes' arm with a pistol shot and grabbed him. Another rioter, David Jones, was shot in the back, cut around the head with cutlasses and then pinned to the ground.

Where did Rebecca come from? There are a number of explanations. Perhaps it alludes to the Biblical quotation from Genesis, about Rebecca and her descendants possessing 'the gates of those which hate them'. A church-going population would have seen the reference instantly.

Perhaps it was a symbolic inversion of the natural order of things, with women (men wearing women's clothes) taking action. A sense of the world gone mad.

Or perhaps it was simply that the first rioter, Twm Carnabwth, borrowed a dress from a neighbour called 'Big Rebecca' from Llangolman. Now that is the explanation that I prefer.

A third, John Hugh, was also captured. It all became, as they say, a bit of a mess. Whilst all this was going on, the troops from Carmarthen over at the Hendy Gate were feeling rather overlooked and eager for action. They marched bravely towards the gunfire, straight into the agitated troops coming in the opposite direction from Pontarddulais. An unfortunate incident in the deep darkness of the night was narrowly avoided.

Another group, from the Stag & Pheasant, led by Shoni Scubor Fawr from Five Roads, decided they must avenge this shameful ambush and went back two nights later to destroy the Hendy Gate. They advanced on Sarah Williams, who managed the gate. She was an experienced collector of tolls – and deeply unpopular. She had been put there to increase tolls, since, unlike others in her profession, she never let anyone pass without paying.

The gate was attacked in the early hours of 9 September 1843. Her possessions were removed from the cottage by the rioters, who burst into her house and then set fire to her roof. And, in the excitable gunfire that surrounded the attack, Sarah was shot. Was it deliberate? It is more likely to have been accidental. Neighbours found her and took her in but she died soon afterwards. She had gunshot wounds to the head and the chest.

There were no witnesses. The inquest jury decided that she had 'died from an effusion of blood into the chest, which occasioned suffocation'. It was a carefully worded verdict which gave everyone a way out.

But there was a sense that enough was enough. Riots and disorder were one thing but the death of an old lady was something else. The attacks faded away and with them disappeared rural Wales' last attempt to assert itself in the face of enormous change.

The remaining threads of the story were tied up in court. Whilst the inquest on Sarah Williams might suggest a certain leniency, this was not always the case.

The Morgan family argued that their excitable reaction to the policemen had been prompted by their mistaken belief that they could not be arrested on a Sunday. Their charges were reduced from assault to misdemeanour. The parents were discharged since they were old and promised to behave, whereas their children received prison terms.

Daniel Lewis was discharged due to the disappearance of the main witness. John Jones, it seems, had fled to America.

Hugh, Hughes and David Jones were transported to Australia and the disturbances died down. A Royal Commission was established and legislation was introduced. But the battle was already lost. Unnecessary gates were removed and tolls were reduced – success, perhaps, for a popular uprising. But they could not hold back the future. Wales became an industrial nation.

AD 1810–1849

WELCOME TO OUR WORLD

THE GROWTH OF industry led to a rapid growth in the population. Swansea attracted the rural poor from west Wales and the west of England, as well as Ireland, Belgium and Germany. Unskilled workers moved quickly into a town without an infrastructure. But for many of them there was no choice to make. Simply relocate or starve.

Children who had no earning power in a rural community could earn a wage in the factories which was greater than that of an agricultural worker. Soon, enclosed working-class communities developed, entirely separated from life on the west side of town. But, of course, demand forced up the price of housing and the town expanded beyond its ability to cope. There was

insufficient water supply. The reservoir built in 1837 in Brynmill was too low to supply any part of the town beyond the station, so drinking water had to come from springs and wells. Not surprisingly, it was still safer and healthier to drink beer than water, just as it had been in Elizabethan times. Conditions were grim, with primitive toilet facilities. Drainage was non-existent. Sewage was discharged untreated into the river.

In 1810 there were complaints about 'the great number of pigs being left to ramble about the streets to the great noyance of the inhabitants'.

In 1815 notice was given by the Corporation to 'John Lewis, butcher, not to suffer any blood or filth to run from his slaughter house to the back part of his dwelling house to Crop Street in the daytime'.

A report to The General Board of Health in 1849, regarding conditions in the town, indicates how little things had changed.

> Bethesda Court is built on a steep hillside and suffers from sewage and filth from the higher levels ... the cottage wall is also the retaining wall of the burial ground and the damp oozes through close to the bedhead.
>
> Morris Lane is one of the worst and dirtiest alleys in the town. Here are 10 houses and no privy.

Our house, in the middle of our street. (By kind permission of the West Glamorgan Archive Service)

A toilet in Mariner Street is described: 'The floor ... is inundated by the liquid contents of the pit,

Rees Court. (By kind permission of the West Glamorgan Archive Service)

Rosser Court, York Street. (By kind permission of the West Glamorgan Archive Service)

so that the seat can be reached only by means of large stones. Another is too filthy to be entered.'

The Sanitary Inspector said: 'In the open street are several dung heaps and similar nuisances and at the back of the Ivy Bush Hotel is a large manure tank requiring immediate attention ... The water springs used by the lower cottagers are defiled by those living above them on the hill.'

These were the perfect conditions for disease to flourish. Cholera is usually water-borne, with flies making their own particular contribution to the spread of infection. There was an outbreak in 1832 when over 300 people died in Swansea and Morriston. It started in and around Frog Street, near St Mary's Church and, just as it did everywhere in Wales, the appearance of this vicious and silent killer boosted attendance at church and chapel.

Health Reports described shocking conditions. There were outbreaks of cholera in 1832 and 1849. After the Public Health Act in 1848, conditions did improve. Some of the worst slums were cleared and new reservoirs at Lliw were built. But sulphuric acid hung in the air and

vast heaps of slag surrounded houses. It was a moonscape. Bleak and dead. One report stated that: 'When pasturing on lands exposed to the metallic fumes, cattle are affected by swellings and abscesses in the feet, premature loss of teeth and paralysis of the extremities.'

Ebenezer Street. (By kind permission of the West Glamorgan Archive Service)

Disease strikes! (LC-USZ62-42547)

The worst parts of the town were at the northern end of High Street and Greenhill Street, known locally as Little Ireland after the refugees from the potato famine who settled there. Dysentery, typhus and typhoid were rampant. It was the centre of the cholera outbreak in late 1849. Improved water supply had helped control the disease by the time of the second outbreak, but there was no water in Little Ireland. It comprised 'old and ill-built houses without drains and with offensive cesspools'. Most of the area has since disappeared, though there are still hints here and there in Mariner Street and Ebenezer Street.

During the second outbreak of cholera, the death of one of the prisoners in the gaol led to policemen washing out the premises with a water engine. Three days later, one of the policemen died from the disease. It took a while, but the connection with water slowly started to form. It was also realised that washerwomen were very 'liable to take contagious diseases' because of their constant use of water.

It was noted that the later cholera outbreak was worse in the areas not provided with water. A line could be drawn across the High Street precisely. Your hopes for survival depended largely on which side of the line you lived.

Slowly, the infrastructure of the town was brought more in line with the size of the population there. But it was never the healthiest of places. The poor hygiene, the industrial pollution and the tendency to wet weather all made the grasp on life quite fragile for some. And, of course, everyone was vulnerable to all manner of exotic diseases from the ships that docked there from around the world.

AD 1865

THE HECLA

LET US START with a grave. Go through the lychgate of St Paul's Church on Sketty Road and you will find a gravestone which is inscribed on both sides. One contains the family details:

Sacred to the memory of William, son of William and Margaret Thomas who died the 29 of September 1865 Aged 25

But if you look at the other side, you will see why his grave is notable. He died of 'yellow fever, caught while working in Swansea at a yard near where an infected ship, *The Hecla* from the West Indies, was lying.' William died in the only recorded outbreak of yellow fever on the mainland of Great Britain.

The Hecla was a modest wooden cargo ship carrying 540 tons of copper ore and 81 tons of copper regulus for the Cobre Mining Co. from Santiago de Cuba. It arrived in the Bristol Channel on Friday 8 September 1865, and picked up a pilot off Lundy Island. The Master reported that he had one very sick man and that he had already lost three of his crew during the voyage. They waited in the Mumbles anchorage overnight and were then towed into Swansea on Saturday 9 September. Men were sent out to support the crew, who were too ill to man the ship properly.

The story emerged in the newspaper, with a short item entitled 'Distressing Shipping News'. The article described *The Hecla* appearing off Mumbles, flying a flag at half-mast. People knew what that meant. Death on board. The crew were paid off and unloading began. Anxious relatives watched as 'one poor fellow [James Saunders] was brought ashore upon a litter [and] died within a few hours.' He was immediately buried. The sanitary inspector reported to the Mayor the news that he had died, apparently of yellow fever.

They realised that they had to isolate those infected but there was nowhere to receive them.

The grave of William Thomas in St Paul's, Sketty. (Author's collection)

'Sitting on the dock of the bay, watching the flies go away.' (By kind permission of the West Glamorgan Archive Service)

Meetings were urgently called 'to prevent any evil consequences resulting from the imprudent step of bringing a vessel into port when so many of its crew had suffered from so contagious a disease'. It was a case of negligence. As the *Cambrian* newspaper said a week later, the desire of the ship's captain to be 'free from his plague prison' and the poor victims to have 'the loving attentions of those gentle nurses whose kindness smoothes wrinkles from the brow of agony' are perfectly understandable, but their exclusion from port should have been essential. *The Hecla* should have gone to a quarantine station at Milford, set up to deal with 'infectious distempers'. But that didn't happen. Once in the dock it was too late. The disease is transmitted by mosquitoes and the weather in Swansea was described as having a 'predisposing atmospheric constitution'. To you and me that means it was hot, of almost 'tropical intensity'.

The weather enabled the insects to survive for long enough to do their work. From 15 September – six days after *The Hecla*'s arrival – until 4 October, twenty people contracted yellow fever. Thirteen died. Numerous others suffered less severe symptoms. It is the only confirmed outbreak of yellow fever on the English mainland. Only a restoration of normal, cooler, weather patterns prevented it from spreading further.

There was a clear sense of alarm at the appearance of this invisible killer. The authorities were anxious to indicate that sanitary arrangements in the town were adequate. A distinguished surgeon, Dr Buchanan, from the fever hospital in London, was sent to Swansea. Public meetings were held. The Mayor was keen to be regarded as doing something. He announced that the ship, the seamen's clothes and the home of James Saunders had been fumigated.

But as people looked for scapegoats, there were rumours that the Mayor was financially involved in *The Hecla* – accusations which he was forced publically to deny. That was the real reason, they said, that the ship had been allowed to dock.

Throughout the press coverage there is an interesting assumption that information should be withheld to prevent public alarm. The details of the symptoms would, we are told, 'be out of place in a newspaper', which is not terribly helpful. It was acknowledged that the people of Swansea were terrified, but the *Shipping and Mercantile Gazette* felt it was all exaggerated. In thirty-four days 'there were but 13 deaths in a population of more than 40,000 which cannot be regarded as a severe death rate'.

And it wasn't only Swansea that was affected. Two of the crew of the *Eleanor* died in Llanelli, more victims of 'this terrible scourge of the tropics'. Their ship had been alongside *The Hecla* in Swansea docks.

The press was very eager to send out positive messages about how the outbreak was managed, because, for a port which relied upon maritime trade, this was a public relations disaster. Swansea was quickly regarded as an infected port. Spain refused to accept vessels and other countries imposed restrictions.

Of course, it ended as quickly as it had begun. Once the weather resumed normal service the mosquitoes died and eventually the story faded from view. But is this our future? Must we one day accept tropical diseases as a symptom of a global village linked by aeroplanes, or as a consequence of global warming?

AD 1788–1937

GOING UNDERGROUND

MINING HAS ALWAYS been a dangerous business and the history of Swansea is littered with underground accidents, injuries and death. There are numerous stories of bodies being brought home at the end of a shift and propped up outside their front door. Miners could die a number of different ways – from earth, water, fire or air. It often seemed only a matter of time before you were singled out to die at work.

'Dad, you haven't washed your hands. I'm telling.' (By kind permission of the West Glamorgan Archive Service)

SCOTT'S PIT, LLANSAMLET, 1788

The pit had been originally opened by Captain John Scott but was abandoned because of water penetration and was subsequently left idle. However, it was restarted after a Cornish beam pump, probably designed by George Stevenson, pumped the water out.

On 14 March 1788, naked lights caused an explosion in the gas-filled mine. Thirteen men and boys were killed.

It was another thirty-nine years before the Davy safety lamp was introduced in South Wales. But, as we will see, they were not always used.

Big John, Big John, Big Bad John. (By kind permission of the West Glamorgan Archive Service)

9 JUNE 1827

'An explosion of fire-damp took place in a colliery in Llansamlet by which 3 men unfortunately lost their lives. We are credibly informed that the Proprietor has furnished the colliery with the Davy lamp but the men, with fatal obstinacy to their own safety, neglect to use them.' (*Cambrian* newspaper)

22 OCTOBER 1831

Four colliers were descending the shaft in a Swansea colliery when the rope broke and they were 'precipitated to the bottom from a height of more than 30 feet and almost 180 yards of rope fell upon them. Three had both their legs and one his arm, broken. One of the men has since died'. (*Cambrian* newspaper)

The Engine House at Scott's Pit, one of the few surviving features of Swansea's coal industry. (Author's collection)

GARTH COLLIERY, CLYDACH, 1849

Twenty-eight-year-old John Jenkins, together with a young boy, was working underground some distance away from his colleagues. There was a sudden roof slip and they were both buried. The boy was trapped in a cavity formed by a large rock falling on their wagon. He could breathe but could not move. He talked to Jenkins, who said that he could feel great pressure pressing down on his head. He began to pray. There was then a second fall and the boy heard Jenkins no more.

The next day, a group of colliers led by Thomas Francis managed to dig the boy out. About two yards further away they found the body of John Jenkins. The only mark on him was a slight bruise to his face.

CHARLES PIT, LLANSAMLET, 1870

The pit began in 1821 and was eventually over 900ft deep. This was one of the most productive mines, producing over 70,000 tons of coal per year by the 1830s. Since the pit was not

Waiting for news. (Author's collection)

THE RHYDYDEFYD PIT, KILLAY, 1872

In 1872, workers dug through into some old mine workings. This was a constant danger in an area like Swansea, which was honeycombed with old mine workings, often unmapped and forgotten. There was a sudden and deadly influx of water, which washed away pit props and caused a roof fall. One man was seriously injured and a father and son were killed – William Bennett, aged forty-two, and his son John, eighteen. They were trapped and suffocated.

THE KILLAN COLLIERY, DUNVANT, 1924

The pit, situated in the west of Swansea, employed 384 men in 1924, producing fuel for the Grovesend Steel and Tinplate works. On 24 November 1924, in an echo of the Killay accident, there was a sudden rush of water which took away roof supports and flooded most of the mine. Rescuers recovered two bodies straightaway but it was clear that others could still be trapped underground. Pumps were brought in and eleven trapped men were brought out alive. They had been in an air pocket for fifty hours. However, three others were missing. Divers were sent down below the

regarded as gaseous, it was considered safe to work with naked lights. But at 5 a.m. on Saturday 23 July 1870, the miners broke into old mine workings; escaping gas caused an explosion, killing nineteen.

In 1864, John Thomas, a collier at the Tir Canol pit in Morriston, was charged with violating the 28th Special Rule. The one about smoking in the pit. John said that he had a copy of the rules; his problem was that the rules were in English and he could only speak Welsh. But even that was less important than the fact he couldn't read at all.

He admitted what he had done: his pipe had exposed the whole colliery to very serious danger. All workers had been warned about the dangers of smoking and the improper use of lamps after a recent explosion at the Morfa pit. They had, in fact, gone there to help get the bodies out. They had all promised not to smoke in the pit ever again. But, of course, perhaps John Thomas didn't understand. Such issues, however, didn't trouble the judge. John was sent to the House of Correction for three months.

---

water level but could find nothing. Eventually, the three bodies were recovered on New Year's Day, 1925.

A memorial to those who died (erected by the Dunvant community) is on the B4296, on the right-hand side towards Gowerton. It is on the path of the woodland walk by the site of the old brickworks, next to the recycling bins.

In a horrible postscript, one of the rescuers, Thomas William, was killed as he went home in the dark. He was hit by a train and decapitated.

WERNBWLL COLLIERY, PENCLAWDD, 1929

The pit was started in 1923 and soon employed 150 men, mostly from Penclawdd and north Gower. On 28 November 1929, the afternoon shift was underground when there was an explosion at 7 p.m. The Loughor rescue team arrived with breathing apparatus and seven bodies were recovered. An inquest could not determine the cause of the explosion, so that part of the pit was abandoned and flooded.

The pit continued to be worked until September 1937. During the very last shift worked at Wernbwll Colliery, miner Sid James was killed by a roof fall.

On Bryn Hir Road, between Blue Anchor and Three Crosses, there is a rather faded memorial to those who died. It is a calm and pleasant place. You can park on the old colliery site and look at wonderful views down to Penclawdd. The simple brick structure tells you, 'We still mourn.'

AD 1914–1918

THE SWANSEA BATTALION

AT THE OUTBREAK of the war in 1914, the Mayor, Thomas Corker, wanted Swansea to be seen as doing its patriotic best, so he promoted a Swansea Battalion in response to Kitchener's call for recruits. A public meeting was held in the Albert Hall on 16 September 1914, and much enthusiasm was generated amongst old men with money, an excess of patriotic zeal, and with little chance of actually having to fight. Money was donated to fund the raising of the battalion. Mr Steer offered a goat as a mascot, though this was rejected in favour of Colonel Wright's bulldog, answering to the name of Tawe.

The young men who would fight were not so easy to find, though this may have been because the minimum height requirement had been set at 5ft 6in and most of the locals were shorter than that. The recruiting office was initially at the Guildhall, and then later at the Mond Building on Union Street. The Commanding Officer was Major Henry Benson, whose family lived in Fairyhill. Even as he took up his duties, he learned that his brother Richard had been killed in France – a reminder of the grim reality of what he was doing.

By October, concern was expressed that recruitment was poor. Consequently, the minimum height requirement was reduced to 5ft 3in, and experienced soldiers up to the age of fifty were now accepted. But progress was slow and there was a sense that young men were apathetic. Appeals were made to them

"TAWE."

Colonel Wright's bulldog. (By kind permission of SWW Media)

to uphold the honour and dignity of the neighbourhood. Eventually, numbers crept up towards 1,000 – but, of course, there were other recruitment options available, not least the navy. Quietly, some concerns were being expressed about the quality of the recruits, as they set off to Rhyl in December 1914 for training. When they marched through Swansea to the station, the reporter for the *Cambrian* said that one was struck by the absence of great enthusiasm on the part of the crowd – but then, perhaps they were more realistic about the horrors that lay ahead.

The Swansea Battalion became part of the 38th Welsh Division and trained in North Wales and in Winchester before leaving for France in December 1915. Once at the front, there were casualties immediately. The first was on Christmas Day 1915, when Thomas Fisher was killed and two others were injured by a shell.

"SWANSEA'S OWN" NEARLY FULL.

ONLY FORTY MORE MEN WANTED.

SOME OF "SWANSEA'S OWN."

An article in the South Wales Evening Post. *(By kind permission of SWW Media)*

Then, on 14 January 1916, Private W. Sandywell died after being accidentally shot by a colleague in the trench. He was a married man with five children.

Poor Lieutenant Devenish died during bomb-throwing training when a live grenade was fumbled by a private and fell to the floor at his feet. The private survived unharmed but Devenish, all the way from Britstown, Cape Province, South Africa, now lies in the Cimetière Nord in Béthune, France.

Families at home began to receive letters like this one, sent to the family of Sergeant A. Kennedy in February 1916:

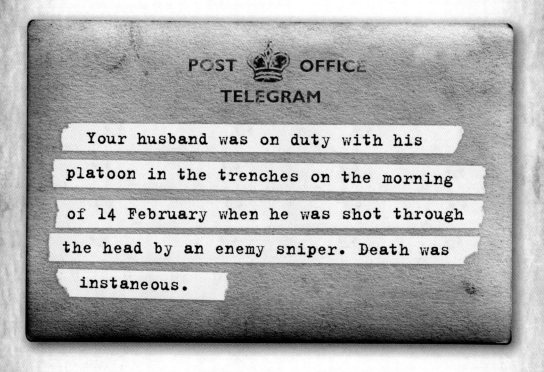

POST OFFICE
TELEGRAM

Your husband was on duty with his platoon in the trenches on the morning of 14 February when he was shot through the head by an enemy sniper. Death was instaneous.

The Swansea Battalion was not involved in the disastrous first day of the Somme Offensive on 1 July 1916, but was selected for duty in Mametz Wood. Fighting in the close and unstructured confines of a wood has always been difficult terrain. You will still find memorials to Mametz in chapels across Swansea.

Preparations had been disrupted by injury. Officers were practising throwing percussion bombs using, for some reason, undetonated live bombs.

*You will find Thomas Fisher in the St Vaast Post Military Cemetery,
Richebourg-l'Avoué, France. (Author's collection)*

*William J. Sandywell is buried in Rue du Bacquerot, No. 1 Military Cemetery,
Laventie, France. (Author's collection)*

*Donald Henry Devenish now rests in Cimetière Nord in Béthune, France.
(Author's collection)*

*The striking memorial to Welsh
soldiers in Mametz Wood, the
Somme, France. (Author's collection)*

They were in two groups, throwing them to each other. And, of course, one went off and there were casualties and a Court of Inquiry. If only they had stopped to consider the paperwork.

The first assault on 7 July 1916 was unsuccessful. Casualties were high and the attack withdrew. They tried again the next day but failed to make progress.

On 10 July, the wood was attacked once again. There was nothing strategic or subtle. It was a case of overwhelming the wood by weight of numbers. The soldiers had to advance in-line straight into well-aimed machine-gun fire. Losses were severe in the pre-dawn gloom. There were no diversions, nothing clever, just a full-frontal assault with close, confused, disordered fighting and death. Bombing had turned the wood into a tangled mess of trees and mud. As you might imagine, it was chaos. One of the battalion said, 'There was little mercy shown by either side.' Sergeant Richard Lyons said, 'Such terms as "Bedlam", "Hell let loose", "The World gone mad" occur to me.' The wood was littered with dismembered bodies.

At the beginning of the day, 676 men of the battalion had advanced on the wood. By evening, ninety of them were dead and 300 wounded. It was deemed to be a success.

Eventually, news reached Swansea. The scale of the casualties must have had a huge impact on the battalion and the town. One of the issues for a battalion like Swansea, with a defined recruitment base, was that it concentrated casualties in one place. The true cost of war was suddenly paid in every part of Swansea. And the transition had been so quick – from civilians to recruits to meat hanging in trees.

The battalion did some work around Ypres burying cables, and took up positions in the mud of the Salient. They fought at Pilckem Ridge and played their part, but never quite recovered from the terrible events of July. In 1918 they came under fire from British Artillery by mistake and twelve men were killed – an early example of the awful concept of 'friendly fire'. But it was for their efforts in Mametz Wood that they have been remembered.

At the end of the war there were celebrations; relief tinged with sorrow. You can understand why the Mayor declined a request from the Temperance Movement to close public houses. There were fireworks. A gun was fired on the beach. And many young men from Swansea remained buried in France.

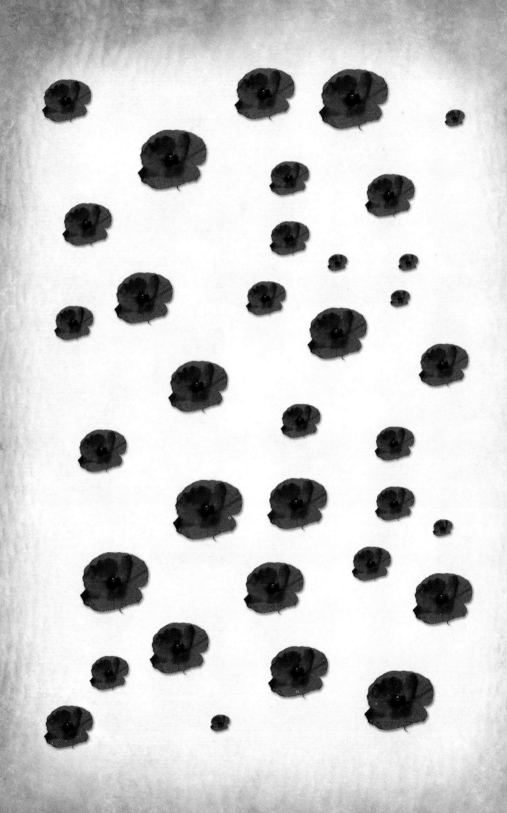

AD 1823–1849

ON THE RIVER

THE TAWE DOESN'T look much today, merely a controlled and tamed river that flows down the valley. But for centuries it was quite a barrier, effectively dividing the town. It was tidal as far as the weir in Morriston, and naturally remained so until the late twentieth century and the development of the barrage. The volume of water in the river depended on the weather in the Swansea Valley. So, although it wasn't very wide, the river was completely unpredictable. It would fall to reveal mudbanks and old wrecks – like the one we all looked at for years in the river at St Thomas – and then rise again and rush down to the sea, taking away litter and debris. There was no bridge across the river unless you went upstream to Morriston, and so further down the valley people relied upon ferries to cross from one side to another. Some would use it on a daily basis, and it was the straightforward route between the east side and the town. It was the route for shoppers who, it is said, would carry furniture like tables and wardrobes down to the river, where the items would be towed across behind the ferry.

But the unpredictability of the river made ferry crossings dangerous.

MELANCHOLY CATASTROPHE, JULY 1823

A party of church-goers were going home after a service in the Calvinistic Chapel in Llansamlet. About thirty of them crammed into the small boat at Foxhole, and they had nearly reached the bank when the boat hit another that was moored at the quay at Pipehouse Wharf. It was reported in the *Cambrian* that, 'This circumstance, though trivial in itself, so alarmed the women that they all rushed to the same side of the boat.' The ferry overturned and threw the passengers into the current, which was flowing rapidly. 'The scene that now ensued was painfully awful: men and women were seen struggling to gain the shore and the shrieks of the latter for assistance were heart-rending in the extreme.'

Ten people were lost, the youngest of whom was George Beddoe, who was six years old. A benefit concert was organised to raise money for widows and orphans.

'I think I will just walk up to the bridge in Morriston, if it's alright with you.' (By kind permission of the West Glamorgan Archive Service)

THEATRE, SWANSEA,—By Authority.

THE Ladies and Gentlemen of Swansea and its vicinity are respectfully informed, that

Mr. GATTIE,

from the Theatre Royal, Drury-lane, is engaged to perform here a few nights.
On MONDAY, the 21st July, 1823, will be presented a Musical Play (never acted here), called

THE KNIGHT OF SNOWDEN;

Or, The Lady of the Lake.
Found'ed on the popular poem of that name, and embracing all its 'eading incidents, adapted to the stage by T. Morton, Esq. with the original Music, new Scenery and Machinery, painted by Mr. Stanton and Mr. Lewis, jun. The Dresses by Mr. Lewis. As performed at the Theatre Royal, Covent-garden, and now performing at the English Opera-House with universal applause.
To which will be added a Farce, called

MONS. TONSON.

The Part of Monsieur Morbleu .... by .... Mr. GATTIE, being his first appearance here these seven years.
On WEDNESDAY, Evening, July 23d, will be presented (for the third time at this Theatre) the New Grand Asiatic Melo-Dramatic Romance (founded on a popular Fairy Tale), called

CHERRY AND FAIR STAR;

Or, The Children of Cyprus.
To which will be added the Historical Drama, called
JOAN of ARC, the Maid of Orleans.
With other Entertainments.
On THURSDAY, July 24, the celebrated Historical Drama,
CALLED

KENILWORTH;

Or, England's Golden Days.
With all the original Music, Scenery, Dresses, and Decorations.
On FRIDAY Evening, July 25, will be presented (for the only time this season) the Extravaganza Burletta of Fun, Frolic, and Fashion, called

TOM & JERRY; or, Life in London.

In Act 5th a splendid Masquerade.
On SATURDAY Evening, July 26th (by desire of the Steward of the Races), will be presented
A favourite Play, Farce, and Entertainments, As will be expressed in future Advertisements.

With all possible deference, the Manager presumes to offer his humble aid towards alleviating the distress occasioned by the melancholy Accident (on the 13th instant), which has called forth the kind and humane assistance of the Ladies and Gentlemen of Swansea in behalf of the surviving sufferers. Mr. M'CREADY respectfully announces a performance at the THEATRE, on TUESDAY next, for that purpose, in the hope that a generous Public will grant their support.
SECOND NIGHT OF
Mr. GATTIE's Engagement.
On TUESDAY Evening, the 22d of July, will be presented
A favourite Play, Farce, & Entertainments.
As will be expressed in the Bills.

Look at the bottom of the advertisement and you can see the announcement of the benefit concert for the victims of the ferry boat disaster. (By kind permission of SWW Media)

MELANCHOLY ACCIDENT, FEBRUARY 1839

The ferry was a commercial venture. There was a licensee who operated it for profit, and health and safety were not always the highest priorities. In fact, in 1839 the state of the ferry was lamentable. Six men were drowned, including the drunken ferryman Evan Morgan at 10 p.m. on a dark Saturday night in February. One of the witnesses was a private ferryman, William Rees, who was operating his own boat at the time (which was in much better condition than the official one). Both boats were propelled by a single oar and needed to be guided across the river on a rope. William saw the ferry set off behind him across the current. The rope wasn't tight enough and the ferry got out of position and became broadside on in the heavy current; it was swamped. William did his best to help and managed to drag some of the passengers into his own boat. However, one of the men, John Jones, held on to the doomed ferry in a panic and this caused William's boat to sink too. William later said:

> One of the men laid hold of my collar and grasped it firmly until we both sank to the bottom of the river; he then let go of his hold and I came up to the surface and swam ...
> I laid hold of some seaweeds and ... came ashore.

It had been a rough night and conditions had been poor. In fact, the official ferry had been unable to operate for about two hours due to the strength of the current. The inquest heard that Mary Howells, from Llansamlet, had turned up to cross but wouldn't risk it. She had taken one look at the boat, the ferryman and the conditions, and decided to walk home the long way round.

What emerges is the fact that the ferry was not seaworthy and neither was the ferryman. The boat was too shallow and Evan Morgan incapable. He was substituting for the regular ferryman who was ill, and when he set off on

> 'All the householders and their families within the Seigniories of Gower and Kilvey are entitled to cross this ferry for customary annual payments. Strangers pay a half-penny each and the customary yearly payment is four-pence for each house. Widows pay two-pence only.
> After ten o'clock at night all persons pay and this is given to the ferryman as a perquisite.'
> (Corporation records)

the crossing he was completely drunk. Everyone had warned him not to try but he was showing off to his mates, with fatal consequences. They recovered his body the next morning from behind the eastern pier.

There had been two ferries, but the larger one had been wrecked when the chain it used (rather than the rope) had broken and the boat had drifted off. So there was only one boat available and it was small, inadequate, filthy and neglected. David Davies, the tenant of the Beaufort Arms Inn, who was also the licensee of the ferry, had been told; he had reported the problem to the steward of the Duke of Beaufort, who owned the rights and was responsible for boats and chains and ropes. But for five months nothing had been done. Nearly 200 passengers used the ferry before breakfast every day. But all of them were taking their lives in their hands.

The inquest jury were alarmed by the negligence of the Duke. They felt that lives should not be placed at risk by 'the caprice of any man, however high in rank or distinguished by birth'.

The Duke was eager to pass on the rights to avoid paying for a new boat, but no one was interested until it was replaced. He eventually agreed to do so 'with as much economy as is consistent with the necessary and fair accommodation of the public'. But in the meantime there were six new widows and twenty-three dependent children under eleven years of age.

DEATH BY DROWNING, JANUARY 1849

George Harris, from St Thomas, fell off the ferry boat and drowned on a Saturday night. He was 'under the influence of strong drink' and fell in when the tide was in and a strong current was coming down the river. His body was found 'slightly disfigured near the spot where he fell'.

AD 1730–1876

ON THE BEACH

TUSKS TAKEN, 1730

On 15 February 1730, the *Shepton Mallet*, of Bristol, homeward-bound from Barbados with a cargo of sugar and 204 elephant tusks, was wrecked at the foot of Pilton cliffs near Worms Head. The crew survived. But the customs men were such a long time coming that the locals were able to select from the goods on offer at their leisure. The tusks proved very popular. The customs men recovered fifty-one tusks and took them to a warehouse in Swansea, but realised that the rest had been carried off. The Swansea customs house had the following notice printed and 'fixed up in ye most publick places':

> This is to give notice to all persons concerned in taking away and concealing or receiving any of the Elephants Teeth, or other goods salved out of the SHEPTON MALLET, of Bristol, lately stranded near Port Inon that if they do not forthwith bring the said goods to the Custom House warehouse, or to Mr Caleb Thomas at Pitton, that they will be prosecuted as the law directs.

A couple of tusks were handed in but the rest disappeared completely.

Tusks. (LC-USZ62-130856)

WHALE MEAT AGAIN, 1761

In March 1761, the people of Llanmadoc were in a state of high excitement. They had spotted something out at sea and thought it was a wrecked boat. They quickly gathered on the shore in anticipation of interesting and easy pickings. The sea was often in the habit of providing such unexpected bonuses. But when the object was eventually washed ashore at Whiteford Point, they discovered that it wasn't a ship at all. It was a sperm whale which measured 65ft long, 17ft high and 7ft 'from eye

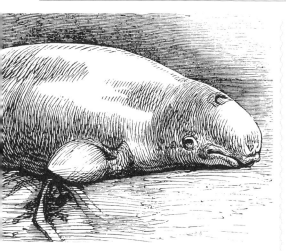

to eye'. It seemed to have a large bruise on its head. When the tide had receded and the poor creature was stranded, they attacked it with hatchets. It took them about five hours to kill.

The steward of Swansea, Gabriel Powell, effectively ran the town for the Duke of Beaufort. As far as he was concerned, the whale belonged to the Duke. It was an asset he should be able to exploit. However, Powell was in Swansea and the whale was on the beach 12 miles away, which made things rather difficult.

By the time he got down there, there wasn't a great deal of whale left. The people of Llanmadoc might not have known what to do with a considerable excess of whale, but it was an opportunity they couldn't ignore. Powell wrote in a letter to the Duke's mother: 'I found about two thirds of it had been plundered and the other third lies buried in the sands, and is now so nauseous that no one will work on it.' You can hardly blame them. A huge pile of rotting whale meat would have raised a mighty stink.

Powell made half-hearted enquiries about the value of whale oil in Bristol but no one was very much interested, particularly since he didn't actually have any to trade. It had all been taken away. He told the local people that if they

brought the meat into Swansea he would make them a decent offer for the oil – but there is no indication that anyone felt the need to oblige.

THE SCANDEROON GALLEY, 1776

The *Scanderoon Galley* was a ship that got stranded in the mud between the streams that run out into the Loughor estuary, probably in the summer of 1776. It carried gold and clearly attracted an element of local interest. The gold was salvaged – except for one chest, which sank into the mud.

Years later, a man from Llanrhidian became inexplicably rich and refused to talk about where his money came from. Then, in the 1860s, the outline of a ship was seen briefly emerging from the mud at Leason Pill. It disappeared again just as quickly in the shifting sands and hasn't been seen since.

BODY FOUND ON THE SANDS, 1876

The body of a child was found near the west pier extension. The *Cambrian* reported that:

> It was in an advanced state of decomposition, the entrails being eaten away apparently by fishes and there was no clothing or wrapper of any kind about it. Mr. Evans, surgeon, made a post mortem examination and gave evidence at the inquest to the effect that it was the body of a child of premature birth, and had been in the water nine or ten days. No evidence could be given as to how it came to the place where found, or whether or not it had been washed ashore and the jury returned an open verdict of found dead.

AD 1864–1876

ON THE ROAD

WITCH ACCIDENT WAS THAT? 1864

Joseph Price, a sixty-six-year-old farmer, was going home to Pennard late on a Saturday night in 1864. He was drunk and managed to overturn his cart. Poor Joseph was found at 2 a.m. on Sunday, 'lying quite dead with his head under it'. A verdict of accidental death was recorded.

But it was also reported that, in December 1862, his wife Anne had died in the same way at the same place. She was regarded, apparently, as a witch and we are told that 'her husband dying as he did has given rise to strange notions of witchcraft among the credulous'. But who in truth could blame them?

FATAL CAB ACCIDENT, FEBRUARY 1873

They held the inquest in the Lamb & Flag on High Street. Poor Ellen Taylor. A sixty-five-year-old widow from Llangyfelach Street in Dyfatty, knocked down by George Sanderson's cab.

The cab had been seen coming along at a moderate speed, carrying Mr A. Willis, a metallurgist from Treboeth, along with his wife and a few friends. George had called out a warning to the old lady but too late, and she was knocked down. Witnesses ran to her, picked her up and took her home, where she later died.

Dangers of the road exemplified!

Sadly, Ellen was very hard of hearing, as well as being short-sighted. Not only that, but she also had a shawl wrapped around her head. Wearing a scarf on a cold February day may have kept her warm, but was not entirely compatible with road safety. The jury returned a verdict of accidental death.

FATAL ACCIDENT IN CAER STREET, 14 JANUARY 1876

The streets of Swansea were narrow and dark. Just look at Green Dragon Lane and you will

1865

An inquest was held in Mile End Workhouse on the body of a newly born female child, the illegitimate offspring of Mary Ann Smith, 'a domestic servant in the family of a gentleman residing in the Mile End Road'. At 2 a.m. on Monday morning, Mary went into labour and was taken to the workhouse in a cab. Sadly, whilst she was waiting for admittance, the child was born in the cab and died. The verdict? 'The deceased died from the want of medical assistance at the birth.' (*Cambrian* newspaper)

Charles Barter, landlord of the Rutland Arms on Rutland Street (now swallowed up by the St David's Precinct), was charged with having unlawfully and cruelly overdriven and abused his horse between Swansea and Mumbles. It was the only horse in harness, pulling an omnibus with twelve passengers at a gallop. Barter was fined 5s, with costs.

see. And this made them dangerous, as Lucy Morgan found out to her cost. Her body was identified by the woman she lodged with – Mary Frazer of Queen Street. Mary saw Lucy alive at 8 p.m. and by 11.30 p.m. she was identifying the body.

Lucy had been close to the Alhambra Wine Vaults, talking to a young man who had turned up to tell her that her brother was dead. She broke off to call to her friend Jemima Hopkins, who was passing by. They stood talking when a cab came down from Castle Square rather quickly. The right-side wheel hit Lucy's shoulder and knocked her down.

The driver, Henry Light, appears neither to have heard nor felt anything. A man shouted after him, 'Stop the cab! It has killed a woman!', but he continued into Goat Street. It was January. It was cold. It was dark and he was all muffled up.

Lucy was picked up and carried into Mr Bulpin's public house, the Vernon Arms in Caer Street, and placed upon a table. There was a lot of blood. It was flowing from her ears, mouth and nose. There was a fracture at the base of her skull and she was quite dead.

The cab had been hired by seventeen-year-old John Bowles, a clerk at Swansea Gas Works, who was going home to Hanover Street with his pal Joseph Cox. They knew nothing about the accident as it had made no impact on them. Unlike Lucy.

The street was quiet, since it had happened before people came out of the theatres. But all witnesses agreed that she wasn't quite on the pavement. Lucy had been standing in the gutter. And even in those days it wasn't the place to stand. The verdict was accidental death and the coroner urged both cab drivers and pedestrians to exercise caution at all times.

AD 1868–1873

ON THE MAKE

WHO WAS WILLIAM Vaughan Bristow?

William Vaughan Bristow announced his new venture in the *Cambrian* in August 1868. He was opening 'a first class school at 25 Mansel Terrace Swansea'. The advert further stated that 'Kindness and patience are the chief characteristics of Mr Bristow's system of education'. It is good to know. He appeared in Swansea from, it seemed, nowhere at all and was clearly intent on dragging the whole place up to date. By November he was writing to the newspapers asking why Swansea wasn't a centre for Oxford and Cambridge Local Examinations. Why should parents take their boys to other towns for these exams? Why not do them here? After all, success in these examinations would be an excellent way for parents to make judgements about schools. Fine and worthy schools (like his own) could be judged against proper national standards and not corrupt local ones. He was even keen to see girls offered the same university education opportunities as boys. Clearly, W.V. Bristow was a man ahead of his time.

He kept on writing to the paper about his system for the Education of the Upper Classes, about school prize day and cricket matches, organising petitions and joining committees. It was part of a carefully judged publicity campaign to promote his school and to promote himself. He was trying to create the impression of an intellectual leader, a man of influence and substance, a mover and shaker within the town.

Soon the school was called Arnold College and then Rugby House, attempting to gain status by association with other, more famous, brands. But his was an image that was hard to sustain. There was an unpleasant hollowness beneath his pretensions, an unattractive skull beneath the skin.

Perhaps others started to sense it too. Bristow summoned William Johnson, the Lloyd's agent in Swansea, over the non-payment of school fees amounting to 4 guineas in August 1871. Johnson had agreed to send his son to Arnold College, but in the event his son became ill and never attended. Bristow demanded payment on the basis that a conversation was in fact a contract. He was laughed out of court and became a figure of fun in the local press. Suddenly, they stopped taking him seriously and soon his reputation was beyond repair.

However, not much was known of his true character until December 1873, when his wife presented a petition for divorce in London on the grounds of his adultery, cruelty and seduction. Unpleasant and sordid details emerged. Fanny

New School in Swansea.

MR. VAUGHAN BRISTOW
(In Honors, London University)

BEGS to announce that he has OPENED a FIRST-CLASS SCHOOL, at 25, Mansel Terrace, Swansea. Kindness and patience are the chief characteristics of Mr. Bristow's system of Education.

Prospectuses and copies of testimonials on application at 25, Mansel Terrace.

(By kind permission of SWW Media)

Just another happy family meal in the Bristow household. (Author's collection)

White had married William on 12 June 1868 and they had lived in Reading where he had been a tutor in a school. They had moved to Bournemouth and then to Swansea. It was in Bournemouth that he had hit her for the first time, in an argument about money. In Swansea, immediately after the birth of their second child he forced her to get up early to make breakfast for the boarders. When she said she was too weak to do so, he threw dirty water over her. On another occasion, he threw a spoonful of gravy at her which scalded her – the sort of behaviour that a clear majority of Swansea's current headteachers no longer endorse.

There were other acts of cruelty too. Immediately after the birth of their child, Bristow made his wife get up and go into the schoolroom to play the pianoforte for the dancing class. Well, supply teachers are so hard to find. Fanny once intervened to prevent him striking their eldest boy, William Charles. He turned on Fanny, dragging her out of the room

and striking her before attempting to throw her over the banisters. Only the intervention of the servants saved her.

There were also other issues. They had a servant called Ferrier who had to leave her work when she became pregnant. Letters from her to Bristow were found (and later reported in *The Times*) in which she 'thanked him for his kindness and said that if he got her a good place near him she would be what she always had been to him hitherto'. A complicated sentence but I think we can see what she meant.

When they left Swansea they went first of all to Kingston, where there were issues about someone called Miss May (who probably did) and, in an argument about the washing, he hit Fanny again. They then moved back to Reading, where William began a relationship with a prostitute, Harriet Webb, who confirmed this in her appearance in the witness box. He also tried to reappoint Ferrier, but Fanny insisted that 'there was not room for two mistresses in the house'. Bristow spat in her face and slapped her. On 20 January 1872 he finally walked out, taking with him what money he could find and their eldest son. It was believed that he had gone to New York.

It is hardly surprising that the divorce was granted. At this point, William Vaughan Bristow disappears from the records completely – so completely in fact that you wonder who he really was. His birth and death are untraceable; he appears to have filled in no census forms. Fanny remarried (becoming Fanny Enever) and died in 1884, aged thirty-seven: our only certain link with the strange William Vaughan. He was a man of self-importance, anxious for status and recognition, anxious to make his mark. But the only lasting mark he made was on his family.

AD 1856–1904

OFF THE RAILS

LANDORE RAILWAY DISASTER, 1856

On the night of Monday 6 October 1856, there was a moment when the railway system in Landore resembled nothing more than a child's train set – but with fatal consequences.

The railways were an essential part of the industrial fabric of the region, moving coal to fuel the factories and running deep into the night. But, on 6 October, the 5.45 p.m. coal train from Neath had a problem in Landore; there was a cattle train on the track and they had to reverse. In doing so they broke a valve and by 9 p.m. they were stuck, blocking the line. The stationmasters managed to divert a passenger train around them. It crept around carefully on the other track, but the line into Swansea remained blocked. The coal train and its twenty-two wagons waited patiently for an engine to pull them away. The guard, Ben West, sensibly displayed a red warning light.

Meanwhile, the 9.45 p.m. coal train was waiting at Llansamlet station for a signal to proceed. The driver, Anthony Allen, and the stoker, Nathan Hedge, were unaware of the situation on the line in front of them and waited patiently for over an hour. They then thought that they received a signal to proceed, so they went down the slope from Llansamlet – and suddenly saw a red light in front of them. The train tried to break but to no avail and, at high speed, Allen – with twenty-eight wagons and 400 tons of metal – ran into the back of the

stationary train just after midnight. There was a fearful mess. Fragments of wagon and engine were scattered everywhere. The force was such that wagons were piled on top of each other. It was estimated that Allen was travelling at over 40mph and was in no position to stop in time, given the incline and the fact that the rails were slippery with rain.

The injuries were serious. Allen was pulled from the wreckage unconscious. He had a severe compound fracture of the left leg and a large lacerated wound to the thigh. His right leg was broken too. The doctors observed him for a while and then decided to amputate the thigh, an operation which was carried out on Tuesday morning. He underwent the procedure successfully but died on Wednesday.

Nathan Hedge was able to give evidence despite his injuries – severe wounds to the head, a broken collar bone and injuries to the lower abdomen. Like Thomas Llewellyn, the guard who had walked away from the smash unscathed, he was adamant that they had received permission to proceed. Who had given that permission? Everyone denied it. Thomas Cannon, the gateman at the crossing in the Swansea Valley, said he'd been told that the second train would perform the same manoeuvre as the passenger train. He said that his supervisor, the Swansea stationmaster, had told him to let the train through on this basis. But no one seems to have told Allen. Communication breakdown is not a new phenomenon at all.

At the end of October, the stoker Nathan Hedge had made sufficient progress to be allowed home to Newnham, near Gloucester. He died almost immediately.

Two Lives Lost and Immense Destruction of Property, 1865

On Wednesday 29 November 1865, the Vale of Neath Railway coal train plunged into the North Dock, killing the driver and stoker.

Coal trains crossed the North Dock in Swansea by a drawbridge. The bridge was open to enable shipping to make use of the tide – but the signalman, John Howells, mistakenly gave a 'line clear' signal. The coal train of thirty-two wagons, driven by William Cole and his stoker Clement Longstaff, could not see that the bridge was closed to them because they were driving backwards. The guard, George Gerrish, leapt off in time but the other two drowned.

John Howells was found guilty of manslaughter and sent to prison for six months. The defence said that he had been exhausted by his working hours – fourteen hours a day, extended sometimes by overtime. And in this context he had made a simple mistake, but a deadly one.

Over 20,000 sightseers went to visit the scene of the accident, paying £40 in tolls which was divided between dependants of Cole and Longstaff. Photographs were taken and sold by Mr Andrews:

> Mr Andrews, photographic artist has taken by the express desire of the company, a series of photographs of the scene of the accident showing all details of the catastrophe which vividly convey the fearful character of the disaster.

Location work by Mr Andrews, photographic artist. (By kind permission of the West Glamorgan Archive Service)

FROM THE OTHER SIDE OF THE TRACKS, 1856

After a good night out on Wind Street, John Jenkins was heading home to Briton Ferry when he was taken all peculiar. So he decided to lie down for a little sleep – on the train line just outside the station. He was found by Charles Anning, Policeman No. 35.

Jenkins was so drunk that he couldn't get up, but PC 35 received no thanks for rescuing him. Instead, Jenkins became abusive and aggressive. Charles later reported that Jenkins threatened 'to scoop my eyes out'. Indeed, he took out a black-handled knife from his pocket. PC 35 watched Jenkins for a while as he struggled with the knife, but the man was so drunk he couldn't open it.

Jenkins had no recollection of the incident and was sentenced to a month's hard labour.

A week later, George Gerrish fell under a guard's van in Port Tennant. He suffered a compound fracture of the leg and died of his injuries.

THE FLYING WELSHMAN, 1904

The train known unofficially as the Flying Welshman left Neyland on Monday morning, with an expected journey time of eight hours to London. In Llanelli, as was the custom, an additional 'bank engine' was attached to help the large train climb over a steep part of the track from Gowerton to Cockett. At 1.21 p.m., and at about 40mph, the whole thing came off the track as it approached Loughor Bridge. The driver of the bank engine, John Lloyd, was hurled from his cab and crushed under its wheels. The fireman, Owen Harries, stayed on the engine to turn off the steam. When the train stopped the funnel broke off and struck him, trapping him in the cab in scalding steam. He died of his burns later in hospital.

Coaches were overturned and three passengers died. Local people joined with uninjured passengers to release those trapped. The injured were taken to Llanelli and Swansea, where onlookers rushed to the station to catch a glimpse of the victims.

The official cause of the accident was 'oscillation' but the people working on the line knew best. John Lloyd had repeatedly told his wife that he wanted another job. This one was dangerous, with the heavier, more powerful train pushing the bank engine along faster than it should.

Within days, postcards of the wreckage were for sale. Swansea Museum have copies you can see, if you ask them nicely.

DECEMBER 1870

Joseph Arthur James, a policeman at the station, didn't turn up to relieve his colleague for his shift at 8 p.m. So his colleagues went to look for him. He was found dead on the tracks, lying face-down with his head towards the Hafod. His head was 'dreadfully cut and he had sustained serious injuries to other parts'. He had been knocked down by the mail train from Milford at 7.50 p.m.

AD 1870

THREE SISTERS AND A HORSE

THE PHILLIPS SISTERS from Halfway in Llansamlet were just fourteen, twelve and seven when they drowned together in Swansea Bay, collecting mussels. Phoebe, Emma and their little sister Amelia were at the beach between Port Tennant and Crymlyn Burrows. Phoebe, who had done it before, took her sisters out to an extensive sandbank called the Dulridge Bank, about half a mile off shore, which at low tide sat about 6ft above the sea.

As you might imagine, when the tide came in they were trapped by the rising water. They were on the wrong side of churning and dangerous currents. The poor girls ran up and down the sandbank screaming as the water rose quickly around them. Their cries were heard by those on the shore. A French sailor, Joseph Corin, managed to swim out to them but he couldn't climb up onto the sandbank. Others tried too. Thomas Enright and another managed to get onto the bank and tried to return with Phoebe, intending then to go back for the others. But the current was so strong that she was torn away from them and sank. The men, exhausted, staggered ashore.

Whilst all this was happening, and as the men looked frantically for a boat, William Thomas, landlord of the Vale of Neath public house, borrowed a horse from Mr Gould, the farmer, and tried to ride off into the tide. The horse refused to enter the water so Thomas had to borrow another. As they struggled through the tide, he was able to grab Phoebe and pull her onto the horse. But the current was too strong. They were both washed off the horse and the poor creature itself was drowned.

All this time her two little sisters were frantic in their terror, screaming for their sister and watching her disappear forever beneath the water. William Thomas made it to the shore 'very narrowly and with great difficulty escaped with his life', according to the *Cambrian* newspaper.

Poor Emma and Amelia were washed away by the tide. As we will see in the next century, these sadly were not the last people lost to the sea whilst collecting shellfish.

All three young bodies were recovered from the local beaches and identified by their great aunt, Tamar Davies. It was agreed that everyone did their best but that the girls had been fatally trapped. A collection was made to reimburse Mr Gould for the loss of his horse, valued at £16.

AD 1914

LANCE CORPORAL WILLIAM FULLER, VC

Our Hero

WILLIAM WAS BORN in Laugharne in 1884, before the family eventually settled in Orchard Street in Swansea. He was not a keen scholar, playing truant from school to such an extent that he was sent to the Swansea Industrial School in Bonymaen. William was clearly a difficult boy and the army was probably his salvation. He joined the Welch Regiment when he was eighteen and served in South Africa and India. On his return to civilian life, he worked as a handler in a timber merchants and then as caretaker at the Elysium cinema in the High Street.

At the outbreak of war in August 1914, William was mobilised. By the end of the month he was back in action (aged thirty) in the front line in northern France. And William lived the dream that failed to bless so many others, since for him the war really was over by Christmas.

He was a private in B Company, commanded by Captain Mark Haggard, and their first act was to join the retreat after the Battle of Mons, which pushed them back across France. They then became part of the Battle of the Aisne. On 14 September 1914, William was promoted to lance-corporal and the company advanced towards the Chemin des Dames, a ridge along which the two daughters of Louis XV rode in carriages in more peaceful times.

Here they came under fire from enemy machine guns outside the village of Beaulne et Chivy. Fuller and Haggard, with two privates, rushed the German positions. The two privates were badly wounded but the attack continued until Haggard was shot and fell to the ground. They were pinned down by heavy German fire and the captain ordered William to retire. He did, running 100 yards or so down the slope. However, it was evident that Haggard was still alive and so William ran back through the enemy fire to his side.

Haggard had been shot in the stomach, with the bullet exiting through the right side of the body. Fuller applied a dressing as well as he could and, as legend has it, Haggard cried out the words that were to become the rallying call for his regiment – 'Stick it, the Welsh!' – presumably a reference to valour rather than Elastoplast.

After an hour or so the fire from the Germans relented sufficiently for William to carry his captain to safety, with Haggard still keen to see a Welsh assault drive the Germans back. With help, William managed to get Haggard back to a casualty clearing station in a barn about half a mile away. Sadly, there was little to be done. Captain Mark Haggard died of his wounds late in the afternoon of the following day.

It was a rescue that fired the imagination, featuring in books such as *Deeds that Thrill the Empire*. There were paintings and engravings depicting the bravery of this ordinary soldier who had been prepared to risk his own life to save that of an officer and a gentleman.

William moved on to Ypres in October. In an advance towards the village of Gheluvelt, he stopped to help a wounded soldier and was hit by shrapnel. He was wounded in the leg and also by a lead ball that went in under his shoulder blade and stopped, narrowly missing his lung and his spine. Evacuated to Britain, William first found himself at a hospital in Manchester and then Swansea, where the ball near his shoulder was removed – allegedly without anaesthetic.

He received the Victoria Cross award as a sergeant on 13 January 1915, and visited the family of Mark Haggard where he met his great-uncle, the novelist H. Rider Haggard. The latter reported that William 'seems to have had enough of it and informed me that his nerve was not what it was, nor his weight either'. William never returned to the front line. As a celebrity, he did what he could for recruitment. In July 1915 he visited Bostock and Wombwell's circus in Fishguard. He entered the lions' cage, casually stroked their heads and, after emerging to a huge ovation, he urged the audience to enlist.

William Fuller, VC. (By kind permission of SWW Media)

William returned to family life in Swansea; to his wife, son and four daughters, and to his job as a man who delivered fish, his life forever defined by those moments in France in 1914. William Fuller, VC died in 1975.

There are two other VC winners with Swansea connections, though neither was born here.

Captain Francis Grenfell was born in 1880 near Guildford. However, his family, owners of the Middle and Upper Bank Copper Works, were major employers in Swansea, and Francis spent extended periods of his childhood at Kilvey. He was awarded the VC in August 1914 in action at Audregnies in Belgium. Killed a year later, he is buried in Vlamertinghe Military Cemetery.

Chief Petty Officer George Prowse was born in Llantrisant in 1886 and the family lived in a variety of locations. He worked at Grovesend Colliery and Mountain Colliery in Gorseinon, and lived initially in Grovesend and later in Landore. Prowse won his VC in action at Pronville in France in September 1918, but was killed three weeks later. His body was never recovered.

AD 1937

COCKLE WOMEN

DYLAN THOMAS SAID they were web-footed. Wynford Vaughan Thomas said they looked like an Old Testament tribe trekking across the desert. Certainly the cockle women of Penclawdd were remarkable.

A regular feature in Swansea market, the cockle women would walk into town barefoot with their boots tied to their waists (to save wear on their shoes) and then stop at Olchfa (which means 'washing place') to wash their feet and put their boots on so as to feel less like country cousins, before marching into town with their baskets on their heads (with a discreetly folded towel beneath their hat as a cushion). When the market was destroyed in the war, the cockle women were among the first to set up stalls outside. Today, Olchfa is the site of Swansea's largest secondary school, but the uniform of the cockle women was much more distinctive with its hats and striped aprons.

They would arrive by train and return on the 2.30 p.m. to Penclawdd, on a train their husbands called The Relish because of the food they brought back for tea. The fact that they earned the money gave them considerable influence, especially in households where the husband was unwell or unemployed. In fact, Penclawdd had a different economy from the rest of Swansea, where a family would depend upon male income. The cockles gave women a real sense of independence. They created a matriarchal society, where boys were not always called after their father. They were no longer Tomos ap Rees

(By kind permission of the West Glamorgan Archive Service)

(By kind permission of the West Glamorgan Archive Service)

LAVER BREAD

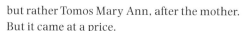

This is Swansea's enduring contribution to world cuisine. Porphyra laciniata: seaweed scraped from rocks, described by some as a green mush. Others do not find it quite so attractive. It has been labelled as an acquired taste, but once acquired it is never forgotten.

Although it was processed in Penclawdd, it was not collected locally. Often it came from the north of England or Scotland. It needs to be picked by hand after the sea has washed over it. In its original form it is wet and heavy, and difficult to carry away over rocks and up cliffs. Definitely a job for someone else. The seaweed is processed in controlled conditions, washed several times, drained and boiled for about eight hours until it looks like treacle – or perhaps the contents of an old lawnmower. You may feel that anything that needs to be boiled for eight hours isn't edible. On the other hand, most things boiled for eight hours could be edible, after a fashion. And yet laver bread is beyond fashion. It is an integral part of the Swansea identity. The need to stuff it into a bacon sandwich is what marks you down indelibly as a Swansea Jack.

but rather Tomos Mary Ann, after the mother. But it came at a price.

It was hard, cold work. The women were out in the estuary in all weathers, day and night. Their hands would be red and swollen from the freezing sand. Their clothes were thick and heavy, and the frost would collect in them on the cold winter days. Sometimes the beds they were working were as far as 10 miles out. The cockles were raked up and then sieved to make sure the smaller ones fell back into the sand. It was back-breaking work and dangerous too. The women developed muscles where perhaps they didn't need them and calloused hands like a miner. They needed an intimate knowledge of local tidal conditions since their hunt for cockles would take them far out into the estuary. Their lives were governed by the tides and they came to know the gullies and the streams because their lives depended on it. But even the experienced could get caught out by the fast-moving tides and their donkeys often drowned in the currents.

In December 1937, fifty-five-year-old Margaret Pamp of New Inn Cottage and thirty-nine-year-old Elizabeth Dallimore of Band Row, both experienced pickers, drowned when the tide rushed in. They had wandered out too far towards Llanelli and couldn't get back. A group of donkeys stopped in the water and refused to move. Six women were unscathed. Four were rescued. The heavy clothes of the unfortnate two held them up in the water for all to see, but their friends couldn't get near them and they were swept away. Their bodies were recovered and they were buried in Penclawdd on 15 December. And we have always bought cockles for just a few pence a bag.

Once collected, the cockles were boiled in large tubs called gypsy boilers and then rinsed in five changes of fresh water. Of course, nothing was wasted. The shells were ground up into grit for chicken feed. Sadly, David Dallimore died when his sleeve was caught in a grinding machine whilst working alone and he was dragged in to his death.

It is hard to associate these tragedies with such an unassuming bivalve mollusc.

DEATH RAY MATTHEWS

International Man of Mystery

IT IS HARD to imagine a more unlikely inhabitant of the Clydach uplands than Harry Grindell Matthews. Scientist, inventor, visionary, spy, self-publicist, nutcase – you decide. His story lives on still on the lonely mountain road from Morriston to Ammanford, where those with a memory shout out, 'Look! That's where he lived. The man who could stop the traffic!' Harry Grindell Matthews. The man who claimed to have invented a death ray.

He was born in 1880 in Winterbourne in Gloucestershire and was, by training, an electrical engineer. Matthews was a man full of ideas, endlessly short of money, and always living on credit in expensive hotels. But he was quite a visionary, working with the hidden powers of radio and light. He transmitted the first wireless press message from Newport to Cardiff in 1912 and then toured the country giving demonstrations, transmitting voice messages between cars. Travelling salesmen today have a lot to thank him for.

He developed the aerophone, a means of transmitting speech to aircraft; the luminaphone, a musical device played by light beams; and a colorscope that could turn voices into a visual display. The sky projector was a particular favourite. This could project an image into the sky and opened up new possibilities for marketing and for fascist rallies (Goebbels was very interested, apparently). His greatest achievement, however, was developing a system for recording sound directly on to film. Matthews was always striving to develop devices controlled by radio beams or beams of light. He had the ideas certainly, but not the technology to put them into practice.

His life coincided with times of war, which made his ideas both attractive and dangerous. When someone claims to be able to activate mines remotely using light beams to release poison gas, dare you risk ignoring him – especially if other countries are interested in him?

He became known as 'Death Ray Matthews' following a short film made in 1924 to promote his new invention. The film suggested that he could use an invisible ray to kill a rat in a cage, stop a bicycle wheel from revolving, and ignite gunpowder. Each an important achievement, in its own way. He featured in an article in the *Sunday Express* in May 1924, 'The man who can make planes fall from the sky', and in 1927 appeared on Pathé News in an item called 'War's Latest Terror'.

However, he would never allow himself to be questioned or tested. Often his equipment never quite worked at demonstration. Many suspected that his reluctance to be put under scrutiny indicated some kind of trickery, that he was merely another eccentric with a mythical device to protect the nation. Matthews saw the requirement to demonstrate and explain his inventions as industrial espionage. But he had little support from his peers. The scientist Ernest Rutherford said, 'Grindell Matthews is best avoided.' In turn, Matthews developed a huge distrust of the government and claimed that other countries

Just another evening of harmless fun with the death ray. (By kind permission of the West Glamorgan Archive Service)

were more interested in his work. This brought the inevitable suggestion that he was a security risk. He was moody and obsessive and eventually bankrupt.

Matthews moved, surprisingly, to Craig Cefn Parc above Clydach, attracted by the solitude that might provide him with trouble-free inventing. His marriage to the Polish-American opera singer Ganna Walska, who had amassed a fortune from her four previous marriages, provided the funding for a house on a remote hillside. He had two acres of land, a tall fence and steel gates. He travelled around in a chauffeur-driven car with the registration GM1 and ate often in the Mason's Arms in Rhydypandy. The bungalow and laboratory Matthews built cost £3,000 and was called Tor Clawdd. It had mains electricity, a generator, its own water supply, private airstrip, housekeeper,

gardener and even, they say, a security guard. He described it as a place of 'space, secrecy and privacy'. Is that why he came to this most unlikely of places?

If you want to believe in conspiracies, you can. The local people did. They said he devoted his time to secret government weapons development. It was bizarrely claimed that a pit that was dug on the mountainside was part of his ongoing work on submarine detection systems. They believed that he was working on his death ray, or on rockets, or on a machine to control the weather, or on germ warfare. Once, the police arrived in response to claims that his 'rays' were causing illnesses among the local population. They remained convinced that he could stop the cars that drove past. They also believed in mysterious visitors. Did German officials come to see him before the war? Did he go drinking with Winston Churchill in the Mason's Arms as some claimed?

Matthews only lived there for three years, but he certainly left his mark and is still spoken about. What was going on? Something? Or nothing? He died on 11 September 1941 of heart failure and was cremated at Pontypridd; his ashes were scattered at Tor Clawdd.

Even after his death the stories continued. It is believed that all his notes, papers and equipment were seized by government agents. American troops were stationed there after his death, in order to guard the site. The locals say so. The Americans deny it, but equipment belonging to the 2nd Infantry Division has been found on this bleak mountain.

Did the Germans try to bomb Tor Clawdd? Bombs did fall up there. Were pilots merely disposing of bombs? Or were they trying to destroy a secret laboratory which they feared?

Hard at work in the laboratory. (By kind permission of the West Glamorgan Archive Service)

Always with Grindell Matthews there are unanswered questions. But at least he can rest assured that his work on bringing traffic to a halt has since been perfected by Swansea city engineers and their roadworks.

Grindell Matthews. (LC-DIG-ggbain-37371)

AD 1940–1943

WHEN HITLER CAME TO SWANSEA

THIS WAS THE last and greatest of all the moments in Swansea's history. The apocalypse. Swansea's armageddon. The Swansea I have written about so far effectively disappeared. The cramped seaport full of narrow streets and ramshackle buildings down to the sea – grubby, claustrophobic and welcoming – was destroyed. Dylan Thomas' 'lovely ugly town' ceased to be. And all because the Germans had it wrong. They were living in the past. Swansea's industry was already in decline. It was no longer such an important hub. And ironically, the docks, the industry and the oil refineries – everything that had brought the bombers – survived largely unscathed. It was domestic life that was destroyed. Why did this happen?

Aerial bombing was notoriously inaccurate, though the Germans were regarded as the most skilled. Their aiming point for raids was Weaver's Flour Mill near the North Dock, which was large and identifiable from the air. The best crews could get their bombs within 300 yards.

That might explain why the bombs seemed to fall upon the tightly packed town. They were not aiming at the town centre deliberately, merely at what they could see from high in the night sky. This also explains why some bombs fell on Kilvey Hill. In fact, 80 per cent of the bombs fell within a radius of 900 yards from Weaver's.

Hitler. (LC-USZ62-97847)

Of course, the bomber crews themselves were terrified. They wanted to drop their bombs and go home as quickly as they could. Precision bombing was not always a priority. And certainly not anywhere near as important as personal survival. They would jettison bombs before they went home, sometimes over the sea. We have found what looks like a crater on Pwlldu Head in Gower. There would certainly be no target here, just a bomb dropped randomly,

---

OUR DEFENCES – DOWN THE DRAIN

On a Saturday in September 1940, the church bells rang – a sign that an invasion was imminent. The Home Guard were called to arms but their rifles and ammunition were locked away in the air-raid warden's post and the Head Warden, with the key, was at home having a bath and couldn't be contacted.

A family outside their Anderson shelter. (By kind permission of the West Glamorgan Archive Service)

perhaps to ensure they went home with an empty bomb bay.

Attacks were expected, of course. Public air-raid shelters had been identified and domestic shelters distributed. Nothing, however, could ever prepare ordinary people for such an assault upon their own homes and lives. A secure and familiar world was ripped apart. The town centre became a shapeless heap of rubble. And the destruction seems gratuitous; without purpose.

The people in this ordinary, unexceptional town, miles from anywhere important, suddenly felt terror and fear. Attacks became part of daily life. For many children it began as an adventure, taking pillows and blankets and candles into the shelter, along with the 'Blitz

GUERNICA

In a strange and rather chilling coincidence, children from the seaside community of Guernica, northern Spain, were evacuated to Swansea to escape the Spanish Civil War and to lodge for a while in Sketty Hall. It was a chance to escape from the *Blitzkrieg* that devastated their town in 1937. The destruction prompted Picasso's famous and disturbing painting *Guernica*, one of the key works of the twentieth century.

And of course Swansea itself was devastated by air attacks during the war. There are those who believe that some of the pilots were involved in both attacks. For this reason, there are many who think that the two places should be forever twinned.

THE FRENCH AIR RAID ON SWANSEA

I have to be honest. It wasn't the French who did it. It was the Germans. But they did it in a captured French plane. Those charged with the defence of Swansea certainly found it very confusing.

It was 10 July 1940, 10.20 a.m., and twelve men were killed and twenty-six injured in an attack on the King's Dock. There was no proper alert because the plane, a Heinkel, carried Allied markings and no one at this time thought the Germans would dare risk a low-flying daylight raid. How wrong they were. The fighter dropped four bombs and then machine-gunned the docks and the surrounding area. It was quite unexpected. It was only the third attack on Swansea and the first time that casualties were sustained.

Bag', which contained valuables and important documents. But they had to experience the sound of the bombs. The smells of the small, confined shelters. They had to go to school amongst all the destruction, the blood, the shrapnel, the dead. They had to deal with losing relatives and friends, with fathers fighting overseas or on constant fire-watch, with disappearing pets.

There were daylight raids too, and the white modern stonework of the Guildhall – such a stark contrast with the rest of the town – was an ideal landmark for daylight raiders. Lone bombers would suddenly appear on a hit-and-run attack, flying low. The purpose of such pirate attacks was to demoralise and breed uncertainty, emphasising the idea that the enemy was invulnerable. They would fly in below Terrace Road, along King Edward's Road, over St Helen's and then out to sea.

People tried to carry on. They made clearly defined roads through the debris, trying desperately to hold on to the world that had been smashed away. But, of course, these extreme circumstances brought out the nutters: those who tried to signal to bombers using tiny torches and mirrors, either to attract them or to blind the pilots. Suddenly anyone unfamiliar or different was a spy.

The town was suffering mass anxiety, and rumours and myths prospered. The shelters were supposedly full of bodies that were hidden and bricked up. The beach was purportedly covered with oil, ready to be ignited in the event of an invasion. There was no planned evacuation of the town. People just left like refugees when they couldn't take any more.

Swansea came under attack on forty-three occasions. The first attack was a raid on Danygraig on 27 June 1940. By the time of the last attack on 16 February 1943, 384 people – our relatives – had died and 859 were injured. It would take many years for the town to be reconstructed; in a new style, for a new age. But the past had gone. As Dylan Thomas said, 'Our Swansea is dead.'

AD 1941

THE BLITZ

THIS WAS NOT the first time that Swansea was bombed in the war – and neither was it the last. But the three consecutive nights of bombing were more than anything experienced by any other town. Coventry, Southampton, Portsmouth, Plymouth and Sheffield all suffered terribly. But only London and Swansea suffered three nights in a row. And for those who lived through those terrible nights, it seemed to be an assault targeted personally on them. Naturally, one of the purposes of the raids was to demoralise the population, though why Swansea should be singled out for such treatment isn't clear.

Heavy raids had already taken place, especially on the east side. The wife of the chairman of the ARP Committee had been killed in a raid. Shelters had been distributed in readiness for more attacks.

The sirens went off at 7.32 p.m. on Wednesday 19 February 1941, and at that moment there was no reason to assume it was anything other than a night-time raid. Within sixteen minutes, the bombs started falling and they continued to do so for over three hours. The other two nights followed a similar pattern. There was a rhythm in the raids, the scale increasing each time, so that on the third night the attack involved at least eighty planes.

Initially there was 'The Demon's Chorus', when parachute flares were dropped to light up the sky. Then incendiaries and high explosives rained upon the town. After three nights, 56,000 incendiary bombs had been dropped

DEALING WITH INCENDIARIES

The front page of the Evening Post *had featured helpful hints about how to deal with incendiary bombs on the very night the raid started. (By kind permission of SWW Media)*

BLACK-OUT
7.6 p.m. to 7.52 a.m.

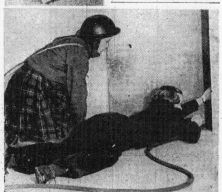

METHODS OF FIGHTING INCENDIARIES were reviewed and demonstrated at a gathering in London yesterday. Top picture is of a woman air-raid warden showing how a fire-bomb should be tackled, and in the bottom picture, a woman is attacking a fire-bomb with a stirrup-pump. Article on incendiary fighting appears in page four.

RATS

Even the rats left the town during the Blitz. They left in a mass exodus up Sketty Road towards Singleton Park. 'They were in a huge black mass that stretched right across the road. The noise of their squeaking was deafening.' (*South Wales Evening Post*)

and 1,200 high explosives. Over 11,000 properties were destroyed, 227 people killed, 409 injured and 7,000 left homeless. On the first night, high explosives were intended to disrupt the infrastructure, damaging gas and water mains, making the fire bombs that were to follow more effective and more difficult to extinguish. In the worst single incident, forty-six people died and forty-four were injured when Teilo Crescent in Mayhill was destroyed.

Help was sent from other towns – Port Talbot, Neath, Llanelli – but rescuers were hindered by craters, rubble, fractured gas mains, and a lack of water. So much water was pumped out of the North Dock that the level dropped by 11ft. Forty-one acres of the town centre were destroyed and the fires that consumed the buildings were seen in Cardiff, Devon and Pembrokeshire.

The BBC said that there was not 'the slightest effect on the morale of the people'. This was not entirely true. People were initially shocked and dazed. Their town, in all its familiarity, had been ripped apart in the dark. They felt powerless, victimised by an unseen enemy. People started to leave town to sleep in tents in Gower and Mumbles. It was called 'trekking'. Whilst the government might consider this 'a symbol of lowered morale', it was merely common sense. It was an action the people could take that seemed so much better than just waiting for the bombs to fall. But the authorities neither acknowledged nor supported what they did. It was apparently regarded as an act of weakness. But it was not. It was a basic survival instinct in extraordinary circumstances.

No one believed the official version of the raids. The destruction seemed too vast, too great to comprehend. Surely the death toll had to be much higher. There were rumours across the rest of Wales that the military had quelled serious civil disturbance in the aftermath, that there had been unrestrained looting. None of that was true. But what is true are the stories of bravery and courage, as people did what they could for each other whilst their senses were assaulted by the screaming bombs, the smell of the fires, and the sight of everything that was familiar melting before them in the strange beauty of destruction.

FROM A SEARCHLIGHT OPERATOR

What puzzled people was that during a raid the lights would go out and the guns would stop firing. This meant that fighter planes were attacking and needed the darkness. So the Germans knew that when the lights went out they needed to head out to sea, jettison their bombs where they could to lighten their load, and get away as quickly as possible.

AD 1939–1945

WE WERE THERE

OF COURSE, INDIVIDUAL stories tell a tale that is much more vivid than a mere outline of events. Here you can hear the voices of Swansea people who lived through it all, recorded at the end of the twentieth century; a wonderful insight into the daily horror that they had to confront. This is where history resides – in the heart and in the experiences of ordinary people. Here are some of the stories they tell:

I was told to take my lanyard off and put it around the knee of the man on the ground. I did, and then tightened the noose so that I had a tourniquet around the knee. He had tried to stamp an incendiary out but it had blown up and he had lost his foot. The blood was everywhere and it was all over my hands and my sleeves.

At long last the van came that was used as an ambulance and just before the van drove away I threw the man's shoe into the inside, and the blood trailed after it, as the man's foot was inside it.

Two young men, firewatching, heard someone crying for help in the dark. They found an old man and took him to a shelter in Brunswick Place, tripping twice over an object in the road. Daylight showed that it was a 500lb unexploded bomb.

In the sitting room behind the shop on the hearthrug there was a ticking bomb. It had come straight down the chimney. The wardens escorted the family to their shelter but the couple in the post office next door refused to move unless an ambulance came to move the invalid wife. Before it arrived the bomb exploded, killing the couple.

As we crossed Oxford Street there was a terrific explosion up towards Castle Street. An unexploded bomb had been put into a lorry ready to be taken away and it exploded killing the bomb disposal team.

It was believed that someone was signalling to German planes with a hand torch from the top of Kilvey Hill. The Home Guard went up the hill and spotted a figure when the German planes released parachute flares that lit up the whole area. They chased him down the hill, firing their rifles after him but he managed to get away.

One man was so fat he could hardly get into his Anderson shelter. During a raid he was so frightened by a near miss that he flung himself inside. He couldn't get out so it had to be dismantled.

We went to a funeral and saw soldiers digging graves. When we asked who they were for, we were told they were ready for the next attack.

I was holding the little girl's hand and we were almost home when the bombs began to fall. I saw a friend who grabbed the girl and they ran into a house for shelter. Suddenly there was a huge explosion. They had run directly into the path of a bomb. They died instantly. I was blown across the road but survived.

Every bomb seemed to be heading for you. My vivid memory is of the dead and mutilated civilians in the Civil Defence mortuaries. Bodies were piled up high prior to mass funerals.

The only way to deal with incendiary bombs was to put a sandbag on it. When a shower of bombs came a young policeman was about to put a sandbag on an incendiary when it exploded. A piece of burning phosphorous went into his mouth and down his throat. To throw water at him would have made the phosphorous burn more fiercely. A sandbag would have suffocated him. We watched him die with white fire pouring from his mouth. [sic]

A flare fell on top of the library. My husband, on leave, went up to put it out. When he came down his smart uniform was covered in melted lead.

Someone was seen flashing a mirror from a hawthorn bush in Sea View Terrace. A group of women chased him to a house in Dyfatty Street. He was obviously frightened to come out and was eventually taken away by the police. There had previously been rumours that the bombers had been guided in by fire on Mayhill.

We all went into Trinity Church for safety but a bomb fell into the crypt and people started to panic and to scream to get out. Luckily the bomb did not explode.

Thanks to the Luftwaffe, from these ruins a place to buy underwear and chicken kievs was born. We thank them still. (By kind permission of SWW Media)

We met an elderly man carrying a small boy. The man was so shocked that he couldn't speak so we took him to the Police Station, only to find that the child was dead.

I had been speaking to Ron, one of the bomb disposal team and I watched him at work whilst dressing the window of Woolworths in High Street. Ron was looking forward to going home to see his wife and children. Suddenly the bomb the team was working on exploded. All were killed.

Suddenly someone shouted he could see a hand. This belonged to a grandmother. When extra help arrived three people were uncovered. Sadly the young mother-to-be and the grandmother were dead, but the little girl was still alive …

These are the words of T.F. Grace, Milton Hopkins, Alex Hendry, Maisie Jenkins, G.J. Dutton, M.B. Thomas and Doreen James, as recorded in *Memories of Swansea at War*, published in 1988 by the *Evening Post* and quoted with their kind permission.

AD 1947

THE WRECK OF
THE *SAMTAMPA*

WHEN THE SEA is calm and the sun shines, the shore is a peaceful place. A place for relaxation and reflection. But it can quickly turn into something else and then we are all vulnerable. The sea is vicious. It respects no one. Lifeboats are no different, and sometimes their luck runs out.

Let us start with a basic outline of the tragedy. The 7,000-ton steamship *Samtampa*, a Liberty ship, had been built in 1943 in America. She left Middlesbrough on 19 April 1947, heading for Newport where she was to undergo a refit.

By 23 April the ship's master, Neale Sherwell, found himself in the Bristol Channel, struggling towards Newport. It was not a good place to be. Gale-force winds were registering 70mph and Sherwell decided to wait for better conditions before proceeding. He tried to drop anchor but the cables were not strong enough to hold the ship in such weather. It was driven, out of control, to the shore.

In only eighty minutes the ship broke up into three sections on Sker Rocks, near Porthcawl. The sea was described by *South Wales Evening Post* as a 'seething cauldron of fury'. The bow and the stern sections were lifted onto rocks just 25ft above the beach. The rest of it, containing the engine room (which was much heavier) was battered continually against them. The crew of thirty-nine died in the wind and the sea and the oil.

Wireless messages indicate that the tragedy happened quickly. The first message came at 3.14 p.m., when the ship sent an urgent signal saying that they were drifting towards shoals. Just before 4 p.m. the signal came that the *Samtampa* had dropped both anchors. But within thirty minutes those anchors had failed and the ship was drifting to the shore. An SOS was transmitted, 'Please send assistance.' The final message was sent at 5.14 p.m., saying, 'Breaking up. Leaving shortly.' Except they had nowhere to go.

The ship carried forty-two lifejackets, but this didn't matter. The *Samtampa* had been driven to the worst possible place. Half a mile to either side and it would have found sandy beaches, where rescue would have been possible. The crew poured oil desperately upon the violent waters around them but it did no good. It created a thick slick through which the victims could not swim. Some tried, but they were either suffocated or smashed on the rocks. None of the bodies recovered died of drowning.

(By kind permission of SWW Media)

93

The tragedy didn't end there. The gun was fired to indicate a ship in distress and the Mumbles lifeboat, *Edward Prince of Wales*, put out to assist the *Samtampa* in mountainous seas at 6 p.m. On a clear day you can see Porthcawl from Mumbles. This was not a clear day. They couldn't locate the ship. The lifeboat struggled for over an hour and then returned to check the position of the *Samtampa*, since they had no radioman on board. They put to sea again, shortly before 8 p.m. This was the last time they were seen alive.

Three years earlier the lifeboat had been triumphant. They had rescued forty-two officers and crew of HMCS *Chebogue*, who were stranded on a sandbar. The coxswain, William Gammon, had received the gold medal from the RNLI. He was the one who took the decision to go out for a second time on this fateful night. He was heard to say, 'I don't think we can make it.' He was right.

No news came to the lifeboat station during the night and the coastguards didn't see it anywhere. The small lifeboat had had to go so close to the shore that it was impossible in the huge waves to turn back and it had been driven

The memorial to the crew of the Samtampa *in Porthcawl Cemetery. (Author's collection)*

inexorably onto the rocks. The coastguards found the lifeboat in the morning, covered, as the *Evening Post* said, 'in wind-blown spray, like a shroud'. It was found overturned at Sker Point, close to the wreck. The crew of eight were all lost. They lie together, still a crew, as they died. You will find them at the top end of Oystermouth Cemetery in Mumbles, in the servicemen's section. William Gammon, William Noel, William Howell, Gilbert Davies, Ernest Griffin, William Thomas, Ronald Thomas, and Richard Smith, who was to be married that weekend. Eight friends and colleagues, forever resting together.

A long procession made its way through the quiet crowds that lined the route to Oystermouth Cemetery in the pouring rain on Tuesday 29 April 1947, and the schools and shops of Mumbles closed as a community gathered together to pay proper respect for families shattered in a selfless act.

The tragedy is remembered in All Saints' Church in Mumbles. There is a beautiful stained-glass window. It was installed in 1977. The boatmen in their bright yellow sou'westers make it so colourful. The wreck of the *Edward Prince of Wales* was burnt.

The crew rest together in Oystermouth Cemetery. (Author's collection)

IN CONCLUSION

HENRY II WROTE to the Emperor of Constantinople:

> There are a people called Welsh, so bold and ferocious that they do not fear to encounter an armed body of men, being ready to shed their blood for their country, to sacrifice their lives for renown.

The historian Gerald of Wales wrote:

> In war this nation is severe in the first attack, terrible in their clamour and their appearance, filling the air with horrid shouting.

Be fair. They are not far wrong are they? To end this brief survey of Swansea, consider this moment from the twenty-first century.

It is Swansea City Centre on a Friday night. A drunken yob, bare-chested, sees men walking past him, dressed in a cartoon version of women – short skirts, high heels, strappy tops and bizarrely coloured hair of absurdly tight curls. These men are clearly an affront to his rigidly constructed world-view. He knows very clearly how men should behave. This is not how men behave in Swansea. He is, as Henry II said, ready to shed his blood for his town.

He mocks them, hurling insults. Yes, as Gerald said, 'filling the air with horrid shouting'. They ignore him. He chases them and swings a punch, 'severe in the first attack'. On reflection, this may be something which he now regrets. Because he had attacked a member of a local cage-fighting team, dressed for stag-night celebrations. And 'They do not fear to encounter an armed body'.

It is over very quickly. In the blink of an eye, our hero is on the ground and his assailant is picking up his handbag and walking away.

It gives you a warm glow, doesn't it? The values of the past still alive today on the Kingsway. But that is Swansea for you, always in touch with its heritage.

BIBLIOGRAPHY

THERE ARE MANY books that have been written about Swansea and I am indebted to many authors much more dedicated and informed than myself. I have used these books during my researches and can recommend them to you without reservation. But I must also confirm that, of course, any mistakes in the text are my own and I apologise for them.

Boorman, David, *The Brighton of Wales* (1986)
Davies, Paul, *Historic Gower* (date unknown)
Dillwyn, Lewis W., *Contributions Towards a History of Swansea* (1840)
Draisley, Derek, *The People of Gower* (2003)
Dulley, Andrew, *The Resuscitation of William Crach* (date unknown)
Foster, Jonathan, *The Death Ray* (2009)
Gabb, Gerald, *Swansea Before Industry: The Town and its Surroundings* (1998)
Jones, William Henry, *History of Swansea and the Lordship of Gower* (1920)
Lewis, Bernard, *Swansea Pals* (2004)
Roberts, Ann, *Estuary People* (2001)
Thomas, Norman L., *The Mumbles – Past and Present* (1978)
Thomas, W.S.K., *The History of Swansea* (1958)
Vaughan Thomas, Wynford, *Portrait of Gower* (1976)